DANIEL BLUM'S

SCREEN WORLD

1958

BIBLO and TANNEN
NEW YORK

© 1958 by Daniel Blum. Reprinted 1969 by
Biblo & Tannen Booksellers & Publishers, Inc.
63 Fourth Avenue   New York, N.Y. 10003
by arrangement with Crown Publishers, Inc.
Library of Congress Catalogue Card No. 70-84068
Printed in the U.S.A. by Noble Offset Printers, Inc.

TO

ETHEL GRANDIN

ONE OF MY

FAVORITE SILENT SCREEN STARS

WITH AFFECTION

AND ADMIRATION

CONTENTS

Assistant Editor: John Willis

Staff Photographers: Louis Melançon, Earle Forbes

Gary Cooper

Yvonne De Carlo

Maurice Chevalier

Joan Blondell

Eva Marie Saint

James Craig

Audrey Hepburn

David Niven

Rossano Brazzi

Anne Francis

Jeff Richards

Ann Blyth

Lauren Bacall

Tony Curtis

Jayne Mansfield

Elvis Presley

6

Anthony Quinn   Lana Turner   Alec Guinness   Sophia Loren

Rita Hayworth   Anthony Perkins   Kay Kendall   Russ Tamblyn

1957 RELEASES

Frank Sinatra   Cara Williams   Anthony Franciosa   Maria Schell

Lauren Bacall, Rock Hudson, Robert Stack,
Robert Keith

8 Center: Robert Stack, Robert J. Wilke

Dorothy Malone, Rock Hudson, Lauren Bacall
Center: Rock Hudson, Robert Keith, Grant Williams

Top: Rock Hudson, Grant Williams (center), Dorothy Malone

(UNIVERSAL)

WRITTEN ON THE WIND

Producer, Albert Zugsmith; Director, Douglas Sirk; Screenplay by George Zuckerman; Based on Novel by Robert Wilder; Costumes, Gowns, Bill Thomas; Assis-

Tom Ewell, Ann Miller, Anne Francis,
Rudy Lee, Mr. Smidgeons

(M-G-M)

THE GREAT AMERICAN PASTIME

Producer, Henry Berman; Director, Herman Hoffman; Screenplay by Nathaniel Benchley; Music by Jeff Alexander; Assistant Director, George Rhein. January release.

CAST

Bruce Hallerton	Tom Ewell
Betty Hallerton	Anne Francis
Mrs. Doris Patterson	Ann Miller
Buck Rivers	Dean Jones
Dennis Hallerton	Rudy Lee
Ed Ryder	Judson Pratt
George Carruthers	Raymond Bailey
Mr. Dawson	Wilfrid Knapp
Mr. O'Keefe	Bob Jellison
Man Mountain O'Keefe	Todd Ferrell
Herbie Patterson	Raymond Winston
Foster Carruthers	Paul Engle
Mrs. George Carruthers	Ann Morriss
Samuel J. Garway	Gene O'Donnell

(M-G-M)

SLANDER

Producer, Armand Deutsch; Director, Roy Rowland; Screenplay by Jerome Weidman; Based on Story by Harry W. Junkin; Music by Jeff Alexander; Assistant Director, George Rhein. January release.

CAST

Scott Ethan Martin	Van Johnson
Connie Martin	Ann Blyth
H. R. Manley	Steve Cochran
Mrs. Manley	Marjorie Rambeau
Joey Martin	Richard Eyer
Seth Jackson	Harold J. Stone
Homer Crowley	Philip Coolidge
Mrs. Doyle	Lurene Tuttle
Charles Orrin Sterling	Lewis Martin

Richard Eyer, Van Johnson,

(PARAMOUNT)
THREE VIOLENT PEOPLE

Producer, Hugh Brown; Director, Rudolph Mate; Screenplay by James Edward Grant; Based on Story by Leonard Praskins and Barney Slater; Costumes by Edith Head; Assistant Director, Richard Caffey; Song by Mack David and Martita; Color by Technicolor. January release.

CAST

Colt Saunders	Charlton Heston
Lorna	Anne Baxter
Innocencio	Gilbert Roland
Cinch	Tom Tryon
Cable	Forrest Tucker
Harrison	Bruce Bennett
Ruby LaSalle	Elaine Stritch
Yates	Barton MacLane
Lieutenant Marr	Peter Hansen
Massey	John Harmon
Asuncion	Ross Bagdasarian
Carleton	Raymond Greenleaf
Maria	Argentina Brunetti
One-Legged Confederate Soldier	Robert Arthur
Rafael	Bobby Blake
Pedro	Jameel Farah
Luis	Leo Castillo
Juan	Don Devlin
Carpetbaggers	Roy Engel, Don Dunning
Maid	Ernestine Wade
Bartender	Paul Levitt

Anne Baxter, Charlton Heston,
Tom Tryon

(UNITED ARTISTS)
THE HALLIDAY BRAND

Producer, Collier Young; Director, Joseph H. Lewis; Screenplay by George W. George and George S. Slavin; Music by Stanley Wilson; Assistant Director, Louis Germonprez; Wardrobe, Irving Leavitt and Patty Page. January release.

CAST

Daniel	Joseph Cotten
Aleta	Viveca Lindfors
Martha	Betsy Blair
Big Dan	Ward Bond
Clay	Bill Williams
Chad Burris	Jay C. Flippen
Jivaro	Christopher Dark
Nante	Jeanette Nolan

Betsy Blair, Viveca Lindfors,
Joseph Cotten

(COLUMBIA)
ZARAK

A Warwick Film Production; Producers; Irving Allen and Albert R. Broccoli; Associate Producer, Phil C. Samuel; Director, Terence Young; Associate Directors, Yakima Canutt and John Gilling; Screenplay by Richard Maibaum; Based on Story by A. J. Bevan; Music by William Alwyn; Songs by Auyar Hosseini and Norman Gimbel; Sung by Yana; Assistant Directors, Jack Martin, Bluey Hill; Photographed in CinemaScope and Technicolor. January release.

CAST

Zarak Khan	Victor Mature
Major Ingram	Michael Wilding
Salma	Anita Ekberg
Biri	Bonar Colleano
The Mullah	Finlay Currie
Hassu	Bernard Miles
Haji Khan	Frederick Valk
Cathy	Eunice Gayson
Ahmad	Peter Illing
Kasim	Eddie Byrne
Moor Larkin	Patrick McGoohan
Sgt. Higgins	Harold Goodwin
Akbar	Alec Mango
Youssuff	Oscar Quitak
Chief Jailor	George Margo
Young Officer	Conrad Phillips

Anita Ekberg, Victor Mature

(M-G-M)

EDGE OF THE CITY

Producer, David Susskind; Director. Martin Ritt; Story and Screenplay by Robert Alan Arthur; Music by Leonard Rosenman; Assistant Director, Don Kranze; Costumes by Anna Hill Johnstone; Associate Producer, Jim Di Ganci; Executive Assistant, Michael Abbott. January release.

CAST

Axel North	John Cassavetes
Tommy Tyler	Sidney Poitier
Charles Malik	Jack Warden
Ellen Wilson	Kathleen Maguire
Lucy Tyler	Ruby Dee
Mr. Nordmann	Robert Simon
Mrs. Nordmann	Ruth White
Davis	William A. Lee
Brother	Val Avery
Detective	John Kellogg
Wallace	David Clarke
Lucy's Mother	Estelle Hemsley
Old Stevedore	Charles Jordan
Nightboss	Ralph Bell

Left: John Cassavetes, Sidney Poitier

John Cassavetes, Jack Warden

Jack Warden, John Cassavetes, Sidney Poitier

Jack Warden
Center: John
Cassavetes

Kathleen Maguire, John Cassavetes,
Sidney Poitier
Center: Sidney Poitier, Jack Warden

Kathleen Maguire
Center: Sidney
Poitier

13

(UNIVERSAL)

ROCK, PRETTY BABY

Producer. Edmond Chevie; Director, Richard Bartlett; Screenplay by Herbert Margolis and William Raynor; Gowns, Bill Thomas; Costumes, Rosemary Odell; Assistant Directors, Ronnie Rondell and Ray de Camp; Music by Henry Mancini. January release.

CAST

Angelo Barrato	Sal Mineo
Jimmy Daley	John Saxon
Joan Wright	Luana Patten
Thomas Daley, Sr.	Edward C. Platt
Beth Daley	Fay Wray
"Ox" Bentley	Rod McKuen
"Fingers" Porter	John Wilder
"Sax" Lewis	Alan Reed, Jr.
"Pop" Wright	Douglas Fowley
"Half-Note" Harris	Bob Courtney
Twinkey Daley	Shelley Fabares
Carol Saunders	Susan Volkmann
Claire Saunders	Carol Volkmann
Kay Norton	April Kent
Lori Parker	Sue George
Mr. Reid	Walter Reed
Bruce Carter	Glen Kramer
Johnny Grant	Johnny Grant
Thomas Daley, Jr.	George Winslow

Geri Wilder, John Saxon, Alan Reed, Jr.

(COLUMBIA)

NIGHTFALL

Producer, Ted Richmond; Director, Jacques Tourneur; Screenplay by Stirling Silliphant; Based on Novel by David Goodis; Gowns by Jean Louis; Music by George Duning; Song by Sam M. Lewis and Peter DeRose and Charles Harold; Sung by Al Hibbler; Assistant Director, Irving Moore; Copa Production. February release.

CAST

James Vanning	Aldo Ray
John	Brian Keith
Marie Gardner	Anne Bancroft
Laura Fraser	Jocelyn Brando
Ben Fraser	James Gregory
Dr. Edward Gursten	Frank Albertson
Red	Rudy Bond
Spanish Couple	Orlando Beltran, Maria Belmar
Bus Driver	George Cisar
Taxi Driver	Eddie McLean

and Lillian Culver, Maya Van Horn.

James Gregory, Anne Bancroft, Aldo Ray

(COLUMBIA)

WICKED AS THEY COME

Producer, Maxwell Setton; Director, Ken Hughes; Screenplay by Ken Hughes; Screen Story by Robert Westerby and Sigmund Miller; Based on Novel, "Portrait In Smoke," by Bill Ballinger; Music by Malcolm Arnold; Assistant Director, Philip Shipway; Costumes, Cynthia Tingey. February release.

CAST

Kathy	Arlene Dahl
Tim	Phil Carey
Larry	Michael Goodliffe
Sam	David Kossoff
Stephen	Herbert Marshall
Dowling	Ralph Truman

and Sidney James, Faith Brook, Frederick Valk, Marvin Kane, Patrick Allen, Gilbert Winfield, Larry Cross, Tom Gill, Alastair Hunter, Anthony Sharp, Raf De La Torre, Pat Clavin, John Salew, Totti Truman Taylor, Paul Sheridan, Frank Atkinson, Jacques Brunius, Guy du Monceau, Selma Vaz Dias.

Herbert Marshall, Faith Brook, Arlene Dahl, Phil Carey

(UNITED ARTISTS)
MEN IN WAR

Producer, Sidney Harmon; Director, Anthony Mann; Screenplay by Philip Yordan; Based on Novel "Combat" by Van Van Praag; Music by Elmer Bernstein; A Security Pictures Production; Assistant Director, Leon Chooluck. Feburary release.

CAST

Lt. Benson	Robert Ryan
Montana	Aldo Ray
Colonel	Robert Keith
Riordan	Philip Pine
Zwickley	Vic Morrow
Lewis	Nehemiah Persoff
Killian	James Edwards
Sam Davis	Al Q. Jones
Maslow	Adam Kennedy
Meredith	Scott Marlowe
Ackerman	Walter Kelley
Haines	Race Gentry
Christensen	Robert Normand
Penelli	Anthony Ray
Lynch	Michael Miller
Korean Sniper	Victor Sen Yung

Aldo Ray, Robert Ryan, Philip Pine

(ALLIED ARTISTS)
LAST OF THE BADMEN

Producer, Vincent M. Fennelly; Director, Paul Landres; Screenplay by Daniel B. Ullman and David Chantler; Story by Daniel B. Ullman; Assistant Director, Edward Morey, Jr.; Music by Paul Sawtell; Wardrobe by Bert Henrikson; Lyrics by Gwen Davis; Filmed in CinemaScope and Deluxe Color. February release.

CAST

Dan Barton	George Montgomery
Ted Hamilton	James Best
Hawkins	Douglas Kennedy
Roberts	Keith Larsen
Taylor	Robert Foulk
Marshal Parker	Willis Bouchey
Green	Harlan Warde
Johnson	John Doucette
Lila	Meg Randall
Dallas	Tom Greenway
Dillon	Addison Richards
Kramer	Michael Ansara
Elkins	John Damler

George Montgomery

(UNITED ARTISTS)
CRIME OF PASSION

Executive Producer, Bob Goldstein; Producer, Herman Cohen; Director, Gerd Oswald; Story and Screenplay by Joe Eisinger; Music by Paul Dunlap; Costumes, Grace Houston. February release.

CAST

Kathy	Barbara Stanwyck
Doyle	Sterling Hayden
Inspector Pope	Raymond Burr
Alice Pope	Fay Wray
Alidos	Royal Dano
Sara	Virginia Grey
Detective Jules	Dennis Cross
Detective James	Robert Griffin
Nalence	Jay Adler
Officer Spitz	Malcolm Atterbury
Chief of Police	John S. Launer
Detective Johns	Brad Trumbull
Detective Jones	Skipper McNally
Reporter	Robert Quarry
Mrs. Jules	Jean Howell
Mrs. James	Peg La Centra
Mrs. Johns	Nancy Reynolds
Mrs. Jones	Marjorie Owens

Sterling Hayden, Royal Dano, Barbara Stanwyck

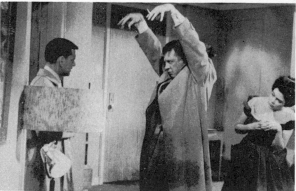

OH, MEN! OH, WOMEN!

Producer-Director, Nunnally Johnson; Based on the Play by Edward Chodorov; Music by Cyril J. Mockridge; Assistant Director, Hal Herman; Wardrobe by Charles LeMaire; Filmed in CinemaScope and DeLuxe Color. February release.

CAST

Arthur Turner	Dan Dailey
Mildred Turner	Ginger Rogers
Dr. Alan Coles	David Niven
Myra Hagerman	Barbara Rush
Cobbler	Tony Randall
Mrs. Day	Natalie Schafer
Miss Tacher	Rachel Stephens
Dr. Krauss	John Wengraf
Melba	Cheryll Clarke
Steward	Charles Davis

Top: Ginger Rogers, Dan Dailey, David Niven

Tony Randall, Dan Dailey, Barbara Rush Center: (L) Tony Randall, (R) Dan Dailey, Ginger Rogers

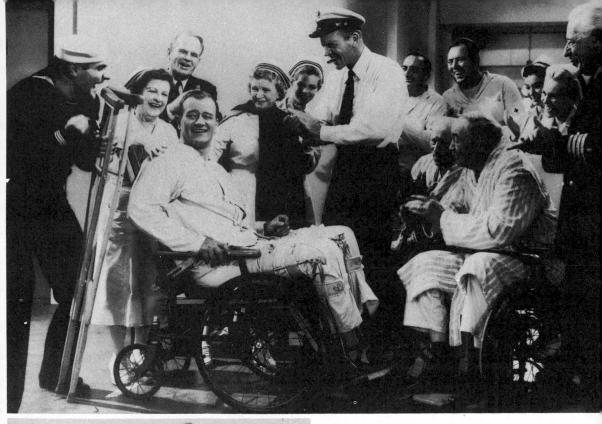

John Wayne, Louis Jean Heydt, Barry Kelley,
Harlan Warde, William Tracy, Dan Dailey
Center: John Wayne, Maureen O'Hara

(M-G-M)

THE WINGS OF EAGLES

Producer, Charles Schnee; Director, John
Ford; Screenplay by Frank Fenton and William
Wister Haines; Based on Life and Writings of Cmdr. Frank W. Wead; Music by
Jeff Alexander; Associate Producer, James E.
Newcom; Assistant Director, Wingate Smith;
Wardrobe, Walter Plunkett; Filmed in Perspecta Sound and MetroColor. February
release.

CAST

Frank W. "Spig" Wead	John Wayne
Carson	Dan Dailey
Minnie Wead	Maureen O'Hara
John Dodge	Ward Bond
John Price	Ken Curtis
Admiral Moffett	Edmund Lowe
Herbert Allen Hazard	Kenneth Tobey
Jack Travis	James Todd
Capt. Jock Clark	Barry Kelley
Manager	Sig Ruman
Capt. Spear	Henry O'Neill
Barton	Willis Bouchey
Rose Brentmann	Dorothy Jordan
Lt. Charles Dexter	Peter Ortiz
John Keye	Louis Jean Heydt
"Arizona" Pincus	Tige Andrews
Pete	Dan Borzage
Air Officer	William Tracy
Executive Officer	Harlan Warde
Joe	Jack Pennick
Aide	Bill Henry
Admiral Crown	Charles Trowbridge
Lila Wead	Mimi Gibson
Doris Wead	Evelyn Rudie
Nurse	Mae Marsh

Top: Tige Andrews, May McEvoy, Louis
Jean Heydt, John Wayne, Mae Marsh,
Janet Lane, Dan Dailey, Henry O'Neill

17

Mallene Hill, Jose Ferrer
Top: Jose Ferrer, Keenan Wynn, Jim Backus

18

(UNIVERSAL)

THE GREAT MAN

Producer, Aaron Rosenberg; Director, Jose Ferrer; Screenplay by Al Morgan and Jose Ferrer; Based on Novel by Al Morgan; Gowns, Bill Thomas; Assistant Directors, Phil Bowles and Ray DeCamp; Music by Herman Stein; Song by Bobby Troup and Leah Worth; Sung by Julie London. February release.

CAST

Joe Harris	Jose Ferrer
Philip Carleton	Dean Jagger
Sid Moore	Keenan Wynn
Carol Larson	Julie London
Ginny	Joanne Gilbert
Paul Beaseley	Ed Wynn
Nick Cellantano	Jim Backus
Eddie Brand	Russ Morgan
Dr. O'Connor	Edward C. Platt
Mike Jackson	Robert Foulk
Harry Connors	Lyle Talbot
Charley Carruthers	Vinton Hayworth
Mrs. Reiber	Henny Backus
Mary Browne	Janie Alexander
Receptionist	Vicki Dugan
Mailboy	Robert Schwartz

Dean Jagger
Center: Keenan Wynn

Top: Joanne Gilbert, Ed Wynn,
Jose Ferrer

Julie London
Center: Jose Ferrer

Bill Travers, Jennifer Jones
Top: Vernon Gray, Virginia McKenna

Virginia McKenna, Jennifer Jones,
John Gielgud

Bill Travers, John Gielgud, Jennifer Jones

Keith Baxter-Wright, Virginia McKenna, Nicholas Hawtrey, Richard Thorp, Maxine Audley,
Kenneth Fortescue, Jennifer Jones, Michael Brill, Brian Smith, John Gielgud

(M-G-M)

THE BARRETTS
OF WIMPOLE STREET

Producer, Sam Zimbalist; Director, Sidney
Franklin; Screenplay by John Dighton; Based
on Play by Rudolf Besier; Music by Bronislau
Kaper; Song by Herbert Stothart; Costumes by
Elizabeth Haffenden; Filmed in CinemaScope
and MetroColor. February release.

CAST

Elizabeth	Jennifer Jones
Barrett	John Gielgud
Robert Browning	Bill Travers
Henrietta	Virginia McKenna
Bella	Susan Stephen
Capt. Surtees Cook	Vernon Gray
Wilson	Jean Anderson
Arabel	Maxine Audley
Harry Bevan	Leslie Phillips
Dr. Chambers	Laurence Naismith
Dr. Ford-Waterlow	Moultrie Kelsall
George	Michael Brill
Octavius	Kenneth Fortescue
Henry	Nicholas Hawtrey
Alfred	Richard Thorp
Charles	Keith Baxter
Septimus	Brian Smith

Jennifer Jones

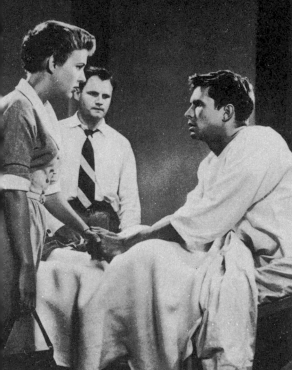

Anthony Perkins, Karl Malden

(PARAMOUNT)

FEAR STRIKES OUT

Producer, Alan Pakula; Director, Robert Mulligan; Screenplay by Ted Berkman and Raphael Blau; Based on Story by Jimmy Piersall and Al Hirshberg; Costumes by Edith Head; Assistant Director, Richard Caffey; Filmed in Vista-Vision. March release.

CAST

Jimmy Piersall	Anthony Perkins
John Piersall	Karl Malden
Mary Teevan	Norma Moore
Dr. Brown	Adam Williams
Mrs. John Piersall	Perry Wilson
Jimmy Piersall as a boy	Peter J. Votrian
Phil	Dennis McMullen
Alice	Gail Land
Bernie Sherwill	Brian Hutton
Joe Cronin	Bart Burns
Radio Announcer	Rand Harper
Bill Tracy	Howard Price
Umpire	George Pembroke
Sandy Allen	Morgan Jones

and Bing Russell, James McNally, Edward Byrnes, Ralph Montgomery, Robert Victor Stern, June Jocelyn, Wade Cagle, Courtland Shepard, Heather Hopper, Mary Benoit, Don Brodie, Richard Bull, Gere Craft, John Benson, Eric Alden, Don McGuire, Marilyn Malloy.

Top: (L) Norma Moore, Adam Williams, Anthony Perkins

(R) Anthony Perkins

Anthony Perkins

(UNIVERSAL)
BATTLE HYMN

Producer, Ross Hunter; Director, Douglas Sirk; Screenplay by Charles Grayson and Vincent B. Evans; Gowns, Bill Thomas; Assistant Directors, Marshall Green and Terry Nelson; Music by Frank Skinner; Filmed in Cinemascope and Technicolor. March release.

CAST

Dean Hess	Rock Hudson
En Soon Yang	Anna Kashfi
Sgt. Herman	Dan Duryea
Capt. Skidmore	Don Defore
Mary Hess	Martha Hyer
Major Moore	Jock Mahoney
Mess Sergeant	Alan Hale
Lt. Maples	James Edwards
Deacon Edwards	Carl Benton Reid
General Kim	Richard Loo
Old Man	Philip Ahn
Gen. Timberidge	Bartlett Robinson
Lt. Hollis	Simon Scott
Korean Official	Teru Shimada
Maj. Harrison	Carleton Young
Capt. Reardon	Art Millan
Navy Lieutenant	William Hudson
Sentry	Paul Sorenson

and children of the Orphan's Home Of Korea.

Top: Philip Ahn, Jung Kyoo Pyo, Anna Kashfi, Rock Hudson
Left Center: Rock Hudson, Anna Kashfi

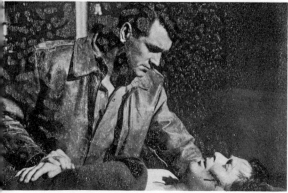

Rock Hudson, Don Defore

(COLUMBIA)

FULL OF LIFE

Producer, Fred Kohlmar; Director, Richard Quine; Screenplay by John Fante; Based on his Novel; Music by George Duning; Assistant Director, Herb Wallerstein. March release.

CAST

Emily Rocco	Judy Holliday
Nick Rocco	Richard Conte
Papa Rocco	Salvatore Baccaloni
Mama Rocco	Esther Minciotti
Father Gondolfo	Joe DeSantis
Joe Muto	Silvio Minciotti
Carla	Penny Santon
Mr. Jameson	Arthur Lovejoy
Mrs. Jameson	Eleanor Audley
Nora Gregory	Trudy Marshall
John Gregory	Walter Conrad
Dr. Atchison	Sam Gilman

Top: Esther Minciotti, Richard Conte, Judy Holliday, Salvatore Baccaloni

Center Left: Judy Holliday, Salvatore Baccaloni

Joe DeSantis, Richard Conte, Judy Holliday Salvatore Baccaloni

(UNIVERSAL)
MISTER CORY

Producer, Robert Arthur; Director, Blake Edwards; Screenplay by Blake Edwards; Based on Story by Leo Rosten; Gowns, Bill Thomas; Assistant Director, Ronnie Rondell; Filmed in CinemaScope and Eastman Color. March release.

CAST

Cory	Tony Curtis
Abby Vollard	Martha Hyer
Biloxi	Charles Bickford
Jen Vollard	Kathryn Grant
Alex Wyncott	William Reynolds
Earnshaw	Henry Daniell
Ruby Matrobe	Russ Morgan
Mr. Vollard	Willis Bouchey
Mrs. Vollard	Louise Lorimer
Lola	Joan Banks
Andy	Harry Landers
Ronnie Chambers	Glen Kramer
The Cook	Dick Crockett

Left: Harry Landers, Tony Curtis, Hylton Socher, Dick Crockett
Top Left: Tony Curtis, Martha Hyer

(M-G-M)
LIZZIE

Producer, Jerry Bresler; Director, Hugo Haas; Screenplay by Mel Dinelli; Based on Novel, "The Bird's Nest", by Shirley Jackson; Music by Leith Stevens; Associate Producer, Edward Lewis; Assistant Director, Leon Chooluck; Wardrobe by Norman Martien and Sabine Manela; Songs by Hal David and Burt T. Bacharach, and Albert Stillman and Robert Allen; A Bryna Production. March release.

CAST

Elizabeth Richmond	Eleanor Parker
Dr. Neal Wright	Richard Boone
Aunt Morgan	Joan Blondell
Walter Brenner	Hugo Haas
Johnny Valenzo	Ric Roman
Elizabeth's Mother	Dorothy Arnold
Robin	John Reach
Ruth Seaton	Marion Ross
Nightclub Singer	Johnny Mathis
Helen Jameson	Jan Englund
Elizabeth (at 13)	Carol Wells
Elizabeth (at 9)	Karen Green
Guard	Gene Walker
Man In Bar	Pat Golden
Waiter	Dick Paxton
Bartender	Michael Marks

Right: Joan Blondell, John Reach, Carol Wells, Dorothy Arnold
Right Center: Ric Roman, Eleanor Parker

(M-G-M)
TEN THOUSAND BEDROOMS

Producer, Joe Pasternak; Director, Richard Thorpe; Screenplay by Laslo Vadnay and Art Cohn, William Ludwig and Leonard Spigelgass; Songs by Nicholas Brodszky and Sammy Cahn; Filmed in CinemaScope and Metro-Color. March release.

CAST

Ray Hunter	Dean Martin
Nina Martelli	Anna Maria Alberghetti
Maria Martelli	Eva Bartok
Mike Clyark	Dewey Martin
Vittorio Martelli	Walter Slezak
Anton	Paul Henreid
Arthur	Jules Munshin
Vittorio Cisini	Marcel Dalio
Countess Alzani	Evelyn Varden
Diana Martelli	Lisa Montell
Anna Martelli	Lisa Gaye
Bob Dudley	John Archer
Tom Crandall	Steve Dunne
Dan	Dean Jones
Girl on Main Title	Monique Van Vooren

Right: Lisa Gaye, John Archer, Lisa Montell, Steve Dunne, Anna Maria Alberghetti, Dewey Martin, Eva Bartok, Dean Martin

Top: Walter Slezak, Evelyn Varden, Anna Maria Alberghetti, Dean Martin

(UNITED ARTISTS)
SPRING REUNION

Producer, Jerry Bresler; Director, Robert Pirosh; Screenplay by Robert Pirosh and Elick Moll; Based on Story by Robert Alan Arthur; Music by Herbert Spencer and Earle Ugen; Song by Johnny Mercer and Harry Warren; Sung by The Mary Kaye Trio; Gowns by Don Loper; Choreography by Sylvia Lewis; Wardrobe by Henry West and Olive Koenitz; Assistant Director, John Burch; A Bryna Production. March release.

CAST

Fred Davis	Dana Andrews
Maggie Brewster	Betty Hutton
Barna Forrest	Jean Hagen
Paula Kratz	Sara Berner
Harry Brewster	Robert Simon
May Brewster	Laura LaPlante
Jack Frazer	Gordon Jones
Mr. Collyer	James Gleason
Miss Stapleton	Irene Ryan
Nick	Richard Shannon
Al	Ken Curtis
Edward	Herbert Anderson
Jim	Richard Benedict
Grace	Vivi Janiss
Mary	Florence Sundstrom
Receptionist	Shirley Mitchell
Sidney	Richard Deacon

and Mimi Doyle, Sid Tomack, George Chandler, Dorothy Neumann, Barbara Drew.

Left: Dana Andrews, James Gleason, Betty Hutton

Center Left: Betty Hutton, Dana Andrews

Deborah Kerr, Robert Mitchum

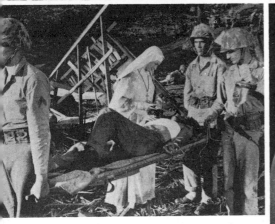

(20th CENTURY-FOX)
HEAVEN KNOWS, MR. ALLISON

Producers, Buddy Adler and Eugene Frenke; Director, John Huston; Screenplay by John Lee Mahin and John Huston; Based on Novel by Charles Shaw; Music by Georges Auric; Costumes by Elizabeth Haffenden; Assistant Director, Adrian Pryco-Jones; In CinemaScope and DeLuxe Color. March release.

CAST
Sister Angela............................Deborah Kerr
Mr. Allison..............................Robert Mitchum

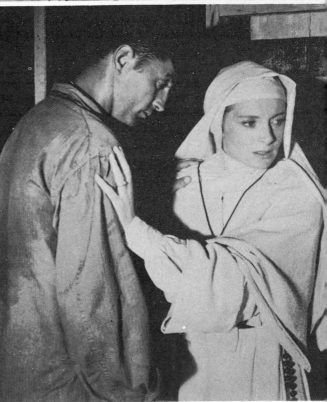

Robert Mitchum, Deborah Kerr

Fred MacMurray, Jeffrey Hunter

(UNIVERSAL)
GUN FOR A COWARD

Producer, Willian Alland; Director, Abner Biberman; Screenplay by R. Wright Campbell; Gowns, Jay A. Morley, Jr.; Assistant Director, William Holland; Filmed in Cinema-Scope and Eastman Color. March release.

CAST

Will Keough	Fred MacMurray
Bless Keough	Jeffrey Hunter
Aud Niven	Janice Rule
Loving	Chill Wills
Hade Keough	Dean Stockwell
Mrs. Keough	Josephine Hutchinson
Clair	Betty Lynn
Chief	Iron Eyes Cody
Danny	Robert Hov
Marie	Jane Howard
Rose	Marjorie Stapp
Stringer	John Larch
Andy Niven	Paul Birch
Durkee	Bob Steele
Mrs. Anderson	Frances Morris

Edward Weston Photo

(CAMERA EYE)
THE NAKED EYE

Written, Directed and Produced by Louis Clyde Stoumen; Music by Elmer Bernstein; Narrated by Raymond Massey; Associate Producers, Gordon Weisenborn and Helen Hahn; March release by Film Representations, Inc. A Documentary film about the fun and art of photography, featuring the photographic life work of Edward Weston and the photographs of Margaret Bourke-White, Alfred Eisenstaedt and Weegee.

Betty Garrett, John Barrymore, Jr.

(COLUMBIA)
THE SHADOW
ON THE WINDOW

Producer, Jonie Taps; Director, William Asher; Screenplay by Leo Townsend and David P. Harmon; Based on Story by John and Ward Hawkins; Music by George Duning; Assistant Director, Irving Moore. March release.

CAST

Tony Atlas	Phil Carey
Linda Atlas	Betty Garrett
Jess Reber	John Barrymore, Jr.
Gil Ramsby	Corey Allen
Joey Gomez	Gerald Sarracini
Petey	Jerry Mathers
Sgt. Paul Denke	Sam Gilman
Capt. McQuade	Rusty Lane
Dr. Hodges	Ainslie Pryor
Bigelow	Paul Picerni
Stuart	William Leslie
Molly	Doreen Woodbury
Girl	Ellie Kent
Myra	Angela Stevens
Husband	Mort Mills
Sgt. Nordli	Carl Milletaire
Bergen	Julian Upton
Conway	Nesdon Booth
Warren	Jack Lomas

Marilyn Monroe
in
"The Naked Eye"

Alfred Eisenstaedt Photo

31

(M-G-M)
THE HAPPY ROAD

Producer-Director, Gene Kelly; Screenplay by Arthur Julien, Joseph Morhaim and Harry Kurnitz; Based on Story by Arthur Julien and Harry Kurnitz; Music by Van Parys; Title Song by Maurice Chevalier; Associate Producer, Noel Howard; Gowns by Pierre Balmain. March release.

CAST

Mike Andrews	Gene Kelly
Suzanne Duval	Barbara Laage
General Medworth	Michael Redgrave
Danny Andrews	Bobby Clark
Janine Duval	Brigitte Fossey
Docteur Solaise	Roger Treville
Helene	Colette Dereal
Morgan	Jess Hahn
Madame Fallere	Maryse Martin
Verbier	Roger Saget
French Motorcycle Officer	Van Doude
Patronne Hotel	Claire Gerard
Armbruster	Colin Mann
Bucheron	Alexandre Rignault
Earl of Bardingham	T. Bartlett
Bicycle Rider	J. Dufilo

Top: Michael Redgrave, Barbara Laage, Gene Kelly
Right Center: Gene Kelly, Bobby Clark, Brigitte Fossey, Barbara Laage

Michael Redgrave, Emerson

(WARNER BROS.)
THE SPIRIT OF ST. LOUIS

Producer, Leland Hayward; Director, Billy Wilder; Screenplay by Billy Wilder and Wendell Mayes; Adaptation by Charles Lederer; Based on Book by Charles A. Lindbergh; Music by Franz Waxman; Assistant Director, Charles C. Coleman, Jr.; in Cinema-Scope and WarnerColor. April release.

CAST

Charles A. Lindbergh	James Stewart
Bud Gurney	Murray Hamilton
Mirror Girl	Patricia Smith
B. F. Mahoney	Bartlett Robinson
Father Hussman	Marc Connelly
Donald Hall	Arthur Space
O. W. Schultz	Charles Watts
Harold Bixby	David Orrick
Major Lambert	Robert Burton
Bill Robertson	James Robertson, Jr.
E. Lansing Ray	Maurice Manson
Earl Thompson	James O'Rear
Commanding Officer	Carleton Young
Farm Boy	Jimmy Bates

James Stewart
Top: James Stewart, Murray Hamilton

33

(20th CENTURY-FOX)

BOY ON A DOLPHIN

Producer, Samuel G. Engel; Director, Jean Negulesco; Screenplay by Ivan Moffat and Dwight Taylor; Based on a Novel by David Divine; Music by Hugo Friedhofer; Assistant Directors, Eli Dunn, Carlo Lastricati; In CinemaScope and DeLuxe Color. April release.

CAST

James Calder	Alan Ladd
Victor Parmalee	Clifton Webb
Phaedra	Sophia Loren
Government Man	Alexis Minotis
Rhif	Jorge Mistral
Dr. Hawkins	Laurence Naismith
Niko	Piero Giagnoni
Miss Dill	Gertrude Flynn
William B. Baldwin	Charles Fawcett
Mrs. Baldwin	Charlotte Terrabust
Miss Baldwin	Margaret Stahl
Chief of Police	Orestes Rallis

Greek Folk Dances and Songs Society.

Top: (L) Alan Ladd, Sophia Loren
(R) Sophia Loren, Jorge Mistral
Left Center: Clifton Webb, Sophia Loren

Alan Ladd, Sophia Loren

Sophia Loren

Lauren Bacall, Gregory Peck   Gregory Peck, Jack Cole, Lauren Bacall

Top: Lauren Bacall

(M-G-M)

DESIGNING WOMAN

Producer, Dore Schary; Director, Vincente Minnelli; Screenplay by George Wells; From a suggestion by Helen Rose; Associate Producer, George Wells; Music by Andre Previn; Musical Numbers and Dances Staged by Jack Cole; Assistant Director, William Shanks; Gowns by Helen Rose; In CinemaScope and MetroColor. April release.

CAST

Mike Hagen	Gregory Peck
Marilla Hagen	Lauren Bacall
Lori Shannon	Dolores Gray
Ned Hammerstein	Sam Levene
Zachary Wilde	Tom Helmore
Maxie Stultz	Mickey Shaughnessy
Charlie Arneg	Jesse White
Johnnie "O"	Chuck Connors
Martin J. Daylor	Edward Platt
Luke Coslow	Alvy Moore
Gwen	Carol Veazie
Randy Owen	Jack Cole

Top: Lauren Bacall, Gregory Peck

Jesse White, Lauren Bacall, Gregory
Peck, Edward Platt
Center: Tom Helmore, Dolores Gray

John Fiedler, Lee J. Cobb, E. G. Marshall, Jack Klugman, Edward Binns, Jack Warden, Henry Fonda, Joseph Sweeney, Ed Begley, George Voskovec, Robert Webber, Martin Balsam

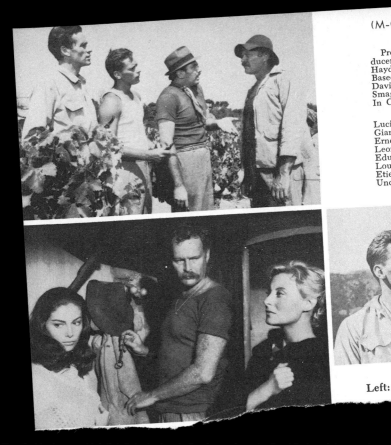

Pr
duce
Hayd
Base
Davi
Sma
In C

Luci
Gia
Ern
Leo
Edu
Lou
Etie
Unc

Left:

(UNIVERSAL)

KELLY AND ME

Producer, Robert Arthur; Director, Robert
Z. Leonard; Story and Screenplay by Everett
Freeman; Gowns, Rosemary Odell; Assistant
Directors, Frank Shaw and Wilson Shyer;
Choreography by Kenny Williams; Filmed in
CinemaScope and Technicolor. April release.

CAST

Len Carmody	Van Johnson
Mina Van Runkel	Piper Laurie
Lucy Castle	Martha Hyer
Walter Van Runkel	Onslow Stevens
Ben Collins	Herbert Anderson
Milo	Gregory Gay
Stu Baker	Dan Riss
Mr. Johnson	Maurice Manson
Dave Gans	Douglas Fowley
George Halderman	Frank Wilcox
Miss Boyle	Yvonne Peattie
Miss Wilk	Elizabeth Flournoy
Joe Webb	Lyle Catell

Van Johnson

Gregory Gay, Van Johnson
Top: Piper Laurie, Van Johnson

Audrey Hepburn (also at Top)

Kay Thompson
Top: Audrey Hepburn, Fred Astaire
Center: Audrey Hepburn

Audrey Hepburn, Kay Thompson
Top: Kay Thompson, Fred Astaire, Audrey Hepburn
Center: Fred Astaire

Top: Audrey Hepburn, Fred Astaire

(PARAMOUNT)

FUNNY FACE

Producer, Roger Edens; Director, Stanley Donen; Screenplay by Leonard Gershe; Music and Lyrics by George and Ira Gershwin; Adapted by Adolph Deutsch; Additional Music and Lyrics by Roger Edens and Leonard Gershe; Choreography by Eugene Loring and Fred Astaire; Assistant Director, William McGarry; Costumes by Edith Head; Paris Wardrobe by Hubert de Givenchy; In VistaVision and Technicolor. April release.

CAST

Jo	Audrey Hepburn
Dick Avery	Fred Astaire
Maggie Prescott	Kay Thompson
Prof. Emile Flostre	Michel Auclair
Paul Duval	Robert Flemyng
Marion	Dovima
Babs	Virginia Gibson
Specialty Dancers	Suzy Parker, Sunny Harnett, Don Powell, Carole Eastman
Laura	Sue England
Lettie	Ruta Lee
Dovitch	Alex Gerry

and Jean Del Val, Iphigenie Castiglioni, Albert D'Arno, Nina Borget, Marilyn White, Louise Glenn, Heather Hopper, Cecile Rogers, Nancy Kilgas, Emilie Stevens, Bruce Hoy, Dorothy Colbert, Paul Smith, Diane DuBois, Karen Scott, Gabriel Curtiz, Peter Camlin, Elizabeth Slifer, Donald Lawton, Karine Nordman, Nesdon Booth, George Dee, Marcel de la Brosse, Albert Godderis, Jerry Lucas, Jack Chefe, Jan Bradley, Jerry Chiat, Elsa Petersen, Fern Barry.

Jack Warden, Philip Abbott, Don Murray   Patricia Smith, Don Murray

Top: E. G. Marshall, Philip Abbott, Don Murray, Jack Warden

(UNITED ARTISTS)

THE BACHELOR PARTY

Producer, Harold Hecht; Director, Delbert Mann; Associate Producer, Paddy Chayefsky; Story and Screenplay by Paddy Chayefsky; Costumes by Mary Grant; Music by Paul Madeira; Assistant Directors, Richard Mayberry and Edward Denault; A Norma Production. April release.

CAST

Charlie Samson	Don Murray
Walter	E. G. Marshall
Eddie	Jack Warden
Arnold	Philip Abbott
Kenneth	Larry Blyden
Helen Samson	Patricia Smith
Existentionalist	Carolyn Jones
Julie	Nancy Marchand
Hostess	Karen Norris
Girl on Stoop	Barbara Ames
Stripteaser	Norma Arden Campbell

E. G. Marshall, Don Murray, Philip Abbott
Top: Don Murray, Patricia Smith

Philip Abbott, Jack Warden, Don Murray,
E. G. Marshall
Center: Don Murray, Carolyn Jones, E. G. Marshall 45

Kathryn Grant, Audie Murphy, Patricia
Livingston, Hope Emerson

(COLUMBIA)

THE GUNS OF
FORT PETTICOAT

Producer, Harry Joe Brown; Director,
George Marshall; Screenplay by Walter
Doniger; Based on Story by William Harrison;
Assistant to Producer, David Breen; Assistant
Director, Abner E. Singer; In Technicolor.
April release.

CAST

Lt. Frank Hewitt	Audie Murphy
Ann Martin	Kathryn Grant
Hannah Lacey	Hope Emerson
Mary Wheeler	Jeff Donnell
Cora Melavan	Jeanette Nolan
Kettle	Sean McClory
Hetty	Ernestine Wade
Lucy Conover	Peggy Maley
Mrs. Ogden	Isobel Elsom
Stella Leatham	Patricia Livingston
Bax	Kim Charney
Salt Pork	Ray Teal
Tortilla	Nestor Paiva
Kipper	James Griffith
Indian Chief	Charles Horvath
Col. Chivington	Ainslie Pryor
Jane Gibbons	Madge Meredith

Albert Schweitzer (center)

ALBERT SCHWEITZER

A Biographical Documentary Feature pro-
duced and directed by Jerome Hill and filmed
by Erica Anderson at Gunsbach, France, and
Lambarene, French Equatorial Africa; Narra-
tion written by Dr. Schweitzer and spoken by
Fredric March; Commentary written by
Thomas Bruce Morgan and spoken by Burgess
Meredith; Presented by Mr. Hill and Miss
Anderson. Dr. Schweitzer's grandson, Philip
Eckart, and his sister, Mrs. Adele Woytt, re-
enact episodes in his life as a boy with his
mother.

William Phillips, Ronald Reagan, Frank
Chase (handing knife to) Robert Arthur

(COLUMBIA)

HELLCATS OF THE NAVY

Producer, Charles H. Schneer; Director,
Nathan Juran; Screenplay by David Lang and
Raymond Marcus; Screen Story by David
Lang; Based on Book by Charles Lockwood
and Hans Christian Adamson; Assistant Director, Abner E. Singer; A Morningside Production. May release.

CAST

Cmdr. Casey Abbott	Ronald Reagan
Helen Blair	Nancy Davis
Lt. Cmdr. Don Landon	Arthur Franz
Freddy Warren	Robert Arthur
Lt. Paul Prentice	William Leslie
Carroll	William Phillips
Wes Barton	Harry Lauter
Charlie	Michael Garth
Chick	Joseph Turkel
Jug	Don Keefer
Admiral Nimitz	Selmer Jackson
Admiral Lockwood	Maurice Manson

(M-G-M)
THIS COULD BE THE NIGHT

Producer, Joe Pasternak; Director, Robert Wise; Screenplay by Isobel Lennart; Based on Short Stories by Cordelia Baird Gross; Song by Nicholas Brodszky and Sammy Cahn; Musical Numbers staged by Jack Baker; Assistant Director, Ridgeway Callow; In Cinema-Scope. May release.

CAST
Anne Leeds	Jean Simmons
Rocco	Paul Douglas
Tony Armotti	Anthony Franciosa
Ivy Corlane	Julie Wilson
Patsy St. Clair	Neile Adams
Crystal	Joan Blondell
Leon	J. Carrol Naish
Hussein Mohammed	Rafael Campos
Mrs. Shea	Zasu Pitts
Stowe Devlin	Tom Helmore
Waxie London	Murvyn Vye
Ziggy Dawlt	Vaughn Taylor
Mr. Shea	Frank Ferguson
Bruce Cameron	William Ogden Joyce
Mr. Hallerby	James Todd

and Ray Anthony and His Orchestra.

Anthony Franciosa, Neile Adams, Paul
Douglas, Julie Wilson

(ALLIED ARTISTS)
LET'S BE HAPPY

Producer, Marcel Hellman; Director, Henry Levin; Screenplay by Diana Morgan and Dorothy Cooper; Based on Play "Jeannie" by Aimee Stuart; Assistant Director, Chris Sutton; Choreographers, Pauline Grant and Alfred Rodrigues; Music by Nicholas Brodszky; Costumes by Anna Duse; In CinemaScope and Technicolor. May release.

CAST
Stanley Smith	Tony Martin
Jeannie	Vera-Ellen
MacNairn	Robert Flemyng
Helene	Zena Marshall
Fielding	Guy Middleton

Robert Fleming, Tony Martin, Vera-Ellen

(UNITED ARTISTS)
BAILOUT AT 43,000

Producers, William Thomas and Howard B. Pine; Director, Francis D. Lyon; Screenplay by Paul Monash; Music by Albert Glasser; Costumes by Alvena Tomin; Wardrobe, Jerry Bos and Fay Moore; Assistant Director, Frank Fox. May release.

CAST
Major Paul Peterson	John Payne
Carol Peterson	Karen Steele
Col. Hughes	Paul Kelly
Kit Peterson	Richard Eyer
Frances Nolan	Constance Ford
Capt. Mike Cavallero	Eddie Firestone
Lt. Simmons	Adam Kennedy
Reinach	Gregory Gay
Major Goldman	Steven Ritch
Capt. Nolan	Richard Crane

Steven Ritch, John Payne, Richard Crane, Paul
Kelly, Eddie Firestone

Katharine Hepburn, Gig Young   Joan Blondell, Katharine Hepburn

Top: Spencer Tracy, Katharine Hepburn

(20th CENTURY-FOX)

DESK SET

Producer, Henry Ephron; Director, Walter Lang; Screenplay by Phoebe and Henry Ephron; Based on Play by William Marchant; Music by Cyril Mockridge; Wardrobe, Charles LeMaire; Assistant Director, Hal Herman; In CinemaScope and DeLuxe Color. May release.

CAST

Richard	Spencer Tracy
Bunny	Katharine Hepburn
Mike Cutler	Gig Young
Peg Costello	Joan Blondell
Sylvia	Dina Merrill
Ruthie	Sue Randall
Miss Warriner	Neva Patterson
Smithers	Harry Ellerbe
Azae	Nicholas Joy
Alice	Diane Jergens
Cathy	Merry Anders
Old Lady	Ida Moore
Receptionist	Rachel Stephens

Top: Spencer Tracy, Katharine Hepburn,
Gig Young, Joan Blondell
Left Center: Spencer Tracy, Katharine Hepburn

Joan Blondell, Sammy Ogg, Katharine Hepburn,
Spencer Tracy, Sue Randall, Dina Merrill

49

(UNIVERSAL)

THE YOUNG STRANGER

Producer, Stuart Millar; Director, John Frankenheimer; Screenplay by Robert Dozier; Music by Leonard Rosenman; Assistant Director, Richard Moder. May release.

CAST

Hal Ditmar	James MacArthur
Helen Ditmar	Kim Hunter
Tom Ditmar	James Daly
Sgt. Shipley	James Gregory
Grubbs	Whit Bissell
Jerry	Jeff Silver
Confused Boy	Jack Mullaney
Man In Theatre	Eddie Ryder
Girl In Theatre	Jean Corbett
Detective	Charles Davis
Mrs. Morse	Marian Seldes
Donald Morse	Terry Kelman
Lotte	Edith Evanson
Lynn	Tom Pittman
Doorman	Howard Price

James MacArthur

James MacArthur, James Daly, Jack Mullaney

Top: Whit Bissell, Kim Hunter, James MacArthur, James Gregory

Kim Hunter, James Daly   James MacArthur, James Gregory
Top and Center: James MacArthur, Jeff Silver

51

(M-G-M)
THE LITTLE HUT

Producers, F. Hugh Herbert and Mark Robson; Director, Mark Robson; Screenplay by F. Hugh Herbert; Based on Play by Andre Roussin and English Stage Adaption by Nancy Mitford; Music by Robert Farnon; Song by Eric Maschwitz and Marcel Stellman and Peggy Cochrane; Costumes by Christian Dior; Assistant Director, David Middlemas; In Eastman Color. May release.

CAST

Lady Susan Ashlow	Ava Gardner
Sir Philip Ashlow	Stewart Granger
Henry Brittingham-Brett	David Niven
Mario	Walter Chiari
Rev. Brittingham-Brett	Finlay Currie
Mrs. Brittingham-Brett	Jean Cadell
Captain MacWade	Jack Lambert
Mr. Trollope	Henry Oscar
Miss Edwards	Viola Lyel
Indian Gentleman	Jaron Yaltan

Walter Chiari, Ava Gardner

David Niven, Ava Gardner

**David Niven, Stewart Granger, Ava Gardner,
Walter Chiari**

David Niven, Ava Gardner

David Niven, Ava Gardner, Stewart Granger

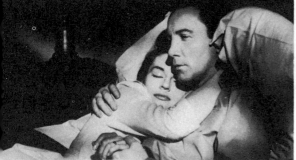

(UNITED ARTISTS)

MONKEY ON MY BACK

Producer, Edward Small; Director, Andre de Toth; Screenplay by Crane Wilbur, Anthony Veiller and Paul Dudley; Associate Producer, Robert E. Kent; Assistant Director, Milton Carter; Music by Paul Sawtell and Bert Shefter. May release.

CAST

Barney Ross	Cameron Mitchell
Cathy	Dianne Foster
Rico	Paul Richards
Sam Pian	Jack Albertson
Noreen	Kathy Garver
Barney's Mother	Lisa Golm
Big Ralph	Barry Kelley
McAvoy	Dayton Lummis
Lew Surati	Lewis Charles
Latham	Raymond Greenleaf
Art Winch	Richard Benedict
Spike	Brad Harris
Dr. Sullivan	Robert Holton

Above: Cameron Mitchell with Jack Woody (top), Kathy Garver (center), Dianne Foster (bottom)

Cameron Mitchell
Top: Charley Green, Cameron Mitchell

(PARAMOUNT)
THE BUSTER KEATON STORY

Producers, Robert Smith and Sidney Sheldon; Director, Sidney Sheldon; Screenplay by Sidney Sheldon and Robert Smith; Assistant Director, Francisco Day; Costumes, Edith Head; Music by Victor Young; Filmed in VistaVision. May release.

CAST

Buster Keaton	Donald O'Connor
Gloria	Ann Blyth
Peggy Courtney	Rhonda Fleming
Kurt Bergner	Peter Lorre
Larry Winters	Larry Keating
Tom McAfee	Richard Anderson
Joe Keaton	Dave Willock
Myra Keaton	Claire Carleton
Buster at 7	Larry White
Elmer Case	Jackie Coogan

and Dan Seymour, Mike Ross, Nan Martin, Robert Christopher, Richard Aherne, Tim Ryan, Joe Forte, Ralph Dumke, Larry Rio, Constance Cavendish, Ivan Triesault, Pamela Jayson, Keith Richards, Dick Ryan, Guy Wilkerson, Elizabeth Slifer.

Top: (c) Donald O'Connor
Center: Larry White, Dave Willock, Claire Carleton

Donald O'Connor
Top: Ann Blyth, Donald O'Connor

Earl Holliman, Burt Lancaster

Rhonda Fleming, Jo Van Fleet

Top: Kirk Douglas, Jo Van Fleet, John Ireland

(PARAMOUNT)

GUNFIGHT AT
THE O. K. CORRAL

Producer, Hal B. Wallis; Director, John Sturges; Screenplay by Leon Uris; Suggested by Article by George Scullin; Assistant Director, Michael D. Moore; Costumes, Edith Head; Music by Dimitri Tiomkin; Associate Producer, Paul Nathan; Song by Dimitri Tiomkin and Ned Washngton; In VistaVision and Technicolor. May release.

CAST

Wyatt Earp	Burt Lancaster
Doc Holliday	Kirk Douglas
Laura Denbow	Rhonda Fleming
Kate Fisher	Jo Van Fleet
Ringo	John Ireland
Ike Clanton	Lyle Bettger
Cotton Wilson	Frank Faylen
Charles Bassett	Earl Holliman
Shanghai Pierce	Ted De Corsia
Billy Clanton	Dennis Hopper
John P. Clum	Whit Bissell
John Shanssey	George Mathews
Virgil Earp	John Hudson
Morgan Earp	DeForest Kelley
James Earp	Martin Milner
Bat Masterson	Kenneth Tobey
Ed Bailey	Lee Van Cleef
Betty Earp	Joan Camden
Mrs. Clanton	Olive Carey
Rick	Brian Hutton
Mayor Kelley	Nelson Leigh
Tom McLowery	Jack Elam
Drunken Cowboy	Don Castle

Burt Lancaster, Rhonda
Fleming
Center: Burt Lancaster

Top: Kirk Douglas, Burt Lancaster,
John Hudson, DeForest Kelley

Jo Van Fleet, Kirk Douglas
Center: Kirk Douglas

ON THE BOWERY

Produced and Directed by Lionel Rogosin, in association wth Richard Bagley and Mark Sufrin; Music by Charles Mills; A Documentary film which visualizes the way of life of men on an American skid row by the projection of one individual (Ray Salyer) during a short period of time. Recipient of Awards from the Venice Film Festival and the British Film Academy. May release by Film Representations, Inc.

Left: Ray Salyer

(COLUMBIA)
ABANDON SHIP!

Producer, John R. Sloan; Director, Richard Sale; Executive Producer, Ted Richmond; Screenplay by Richard Sale; Music by Sir Arthur Bliss; Assistant Director, Basil Keys; A Copa Production. May release.

CAST

Alec Holmes	Tyrone Power
Julie	Mai Zetterling
Frank Kelly	Lloyd Nolan
Will McKinley	Stephen Boyd
Edith Middleton	Moira Lister
"Cookie" Morrow	James Hayter
Mrs. Knudsen	Marie Lohr
Daniel Cane	Moultrie Kelsall
Aubrey Clark	Noel Willman
John Merritt	Gordon Jackson
Maj. Gen. Barrington	Clive Morton
Capt. Darrow	Laurence Naismith
"Sparks" Clary	John Stratton
Willy Hawkins	Victor Maddern
Michael Faroni	Eddie Byrne
John Hayden	David Langton

and Ralph Michael, Orlando Martins, Jill Melford, Ferdy Mayne, Clare Austin, Danny Green, Derek Sydney, Austin Trevor, Colin Broadley, John Gray, Meurig Wyn-Jones.

Right Center: (in water) Austin Trevor, Orlando Martins, Mai Zetterling, Tyrone Power, (in boat) Laurence Naismith, James Hayter, Marie Lohr, Danny Green, Gordon Jackson, Clive Morton, John Stratton, John Gray, Moira Lister, Ferdy Mayne, David Langton, Jill Melford, Eddie Byrne, Noel Willman, Stephen Boyd

Tyrone Power, Marie Lohr, Clive Morton, Gordon Jackson

(M-G-M)

TARZAN AND
THE LOST SAFARI

A Sol Lesser Presentation; Producer, John Croydon; Director, Bruce Humberstone; Screenplay by Montgomery Pittman and Lillie Hayward; Based on characters created by Edgar Rice Burroughs; Music by Clifton Parker; Assistant Director, F. Slark; Dress Designer, Anna Duse; Dances by Harold Holness; Executive Producer, N. Peter Rathvon; In Technicolor. May release.

CAST

Tarzan	Gordon Scott
"Tusker" Hawkins	Robert Beatty
Gamage Dean	Yolande Donlan
Diana Penrod	Betta St. John
"Doodles" Fletcher	Wilfrid Hyde White
Carl Kraski	George Coulouris
Dick Penrod	Peter Arne
Chief Ogonooro	Orlando Martins

and Cheta.

Betta St. John, Peter Arne
Top and Center: Gordon
Scott, Yolande Donlan

Gordon Scott, Betta St. John
Top: George Coulouris, Yolande Donlan, Peter
Arne, Wilfrid Hyde White, Gordon Scott

59

(COLUMBIA)

THE STRANGE ONE

Producer, Sam Spiegel; Director, Jack Garfein; Screenplay by Calder Willingham; Based on his Novel and Play, "End As A Man"; Assistant Directors, Arthur Steckler, Jack Grossberg; Music by Kenyon Hopkins; A Horizon Production. May release.

CAST

Jocko De Paris	Ben Gazzara
Harold Knoble	Pat Hingle
Cadet Colonel Corger	Mark Richman
Simmons	Arthur Storch
Perrin McKee	Paul E. Richards
Major Avery	Larry Gates
Colonel Ramey	Clifton James
Georgie Avery	Geoffrey Horne
Roger Gatt	James Olson
Rosebud	Julie Wilson
Robert Marquales	George Peppard

Ben Gazzara

Geoffrey Horne
Top: Ben Gazzara, George Peppard, Arthur Storch

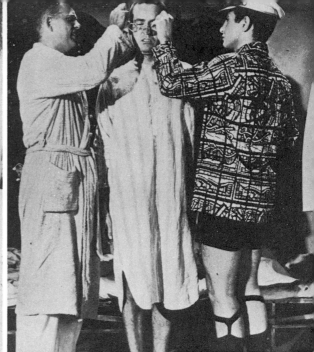

George Peppard, James Olson, Arthur Storch, Ben
Gazzara, Pat Hingle; Top: Ben Gazzara, Mark
Richman, James Olson; Center: Ben Gazzara,
Paul Richards

Ben Gazzara, Julie Wilson
Top: Pat Hingle, Arthur Storch, Ben Gazzara
Center: Ben Gazzara, George Peppard,
Arthur Storch

(UNIVERSAL)

PUBLIC PIGEON NO. 1

Producer, Harry Tugend; Director, Norman Z. McLeon; Screenplay by Harry Tugend; Based on Story by Don Quinn and Larry Berns; From a Teleplay by Devery Freeman; Music by David Rose; Songs by Matty Malneck and Eve Marley; Sung by Vivian Blaine; Assistant Director, Ben Chapman; Choreographer, Miriam Nelson; Costumes by Bernice Pontrelli; A Val-Ritchie Production; An RKO picture in Technicolor. June release.

CAST

Rusty Morgan	Red Skelton
Rita DeLacey	Vivian Blaine
Edith Enders	Janet Blair
Lt. Ross Qualen	Jay C. Flippen
Harvey Baker	Allyn Joslyn
Frankie Frannis	Benny Baker
Avery	Milton Frome
Dipso Dave Rutherford	John Abbott
Warden	Howard McNear
Harrigan	James Burke
Club Manager	Herg Vigran
The Seven Ashtons	

Red Skelton, John Abbott, Vivian Blaine

Top: Benny Baker, Allyn Joslyn, Red Skelton, Vivian Blaine
Left Center: Janet Blair, Red Skelton

(20th CENTURY-FOX)
THE WAYWARD BUS

Producer, Charles Brackett; Director, Victor Vicas; Screenplay by Ivan Moffat; Based on Novel by John Steinbeck; Music by Leigh Harline; Wardrobe, Charles LeMaire; Costumes, Mary Wills; Assistant Director, William Eckhardt; In CinemaScope. June release.

CAST

Alice	Joan Collins
Camille	Jayne Mansfield
Ernest Horton	Dan Dailey
Johnny Chicoy	Rick Jason
Norma	Betty Lou Keim
Mildred Pritchard	Dolores Michaels
Pritchard	Larry Keating
Morse	Robert Bray
Mrs. Pritchard	Kathryn Givney
Pimples	Dee Pollock
Van Brunt	Will Wright

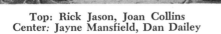

Top: Rick Jason, Joan Collins
Center: Jayne Mansfield, Dan Dailey

Rick Jason, Betty Lou Keim, Dee Pollock

Anton Walbrook, Richard Todd, Jean Seberg

Richard Todd, Jean Seberg

Richard Widmark, Jean Seberg

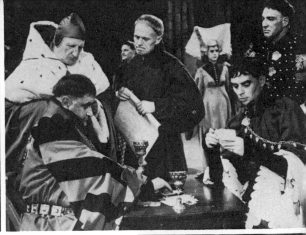

(UNITED ARTISTS)
SAINT JOAN

Producer-Director, Otto Preminger; Screen play by Graham Greene; Based on Bernard Shaw's Play; Music by Mischa Spoliansky; Associate Producer, Douglas Peirce; Assistant Director, Peter Bolton; Production Design, Roger Furse. June release.

CAST

Joan	Jean Seberg
The Dauphin	Richard Widmark
Dunois	Richard Todd
Cauchon, Bishop of Beauvais	Anton Walbrook
The Earl of Warwick	John Gielgud
The Inquisitor	Felix Aylmer
John de Stogumber	Harry Andrews
de Courcelles	Barry Jones
The Archbishop of Rheims	Finlay Currie
The Master Executioner	Bernard Miles
Captain la Hire	Patrick Barr
Brother Martin Ladvenu	Kenneth Haigh
Robert de Beaudricourt	Archie Duncan
Duchesse de la Tremouille	Margot Grahame
La Tremouille, Lord Chamberlain	Francis De Wolff
English Soldier	Victor Maddern
Bluebeard, Gilles de Rais	David Oxley
The Steward	Sydney Bromley
Warwick's Officer	David Langton

Richard Widmark

Jean Seberg

Jean Seberg, Kenneth Haigh
Top: Jean Seberg, Kenneth Haigh, Felix Aylmer, Barry Jones

Harry Andrews, John Gielgud

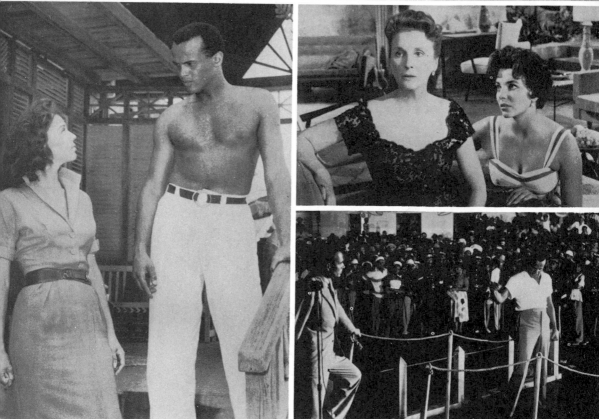

Dorothy Dandridge, Harry Belafonte
Top: Joan Collins, Stephen Boyd

James Mason, Harry Belafonte
Center: Diana Wynyard, Joan Collins

66

(20th CENTURY-FOX)
ISLAND IN THE SUN

Producer, Darryl F. Zanuck; Director, Robert Rossen; Screenplay by Alfred Hayes; Based on Novel by Alec Waugh; Music by Malcolm Arnold; Assistant Director, Gerry O'Hara; Costumes by David Ffolkes; In CinemaScope and DeLuxe Color. June release.

CAST

Maxwell Fleury	James Mason
Mavis	Joan Fontaine
Margot Seaton	Dorothy Dandridge
Jocelyn	Joan Collins
Hilary Carson	Michael Rennie
Mrs. Fleury	Diana Wynyard
Col. Whittingham	John Williams
Euan Templeton	Stephen Boyd
Sylvia	Patricia Owens
Julian Fleury	Basil Sydney
David Archer	John Justin
The Governor	Ronald Squire
Bradshaw	Hartley Power
David Boyeur	Harry Belafonte

John Williams, James Mason
Top: Harry Belafonte, Joan Fontaine

Top: John Justin, Dorothy Dandridge
Center: Patricia Owens, James Mason, Michael Rennie

67

(WARNER BROS.)
THE D.I.

Producer-Director, Jack Webb; Assistant Director, Harry D'Arcy; Screenplay by James Lee Barrett; Music by David Buttolph; Wardrobe, Maxwell Shieff and Alex Velcoff; Song by Ray Coniff and Fred Weismantel; A Mark VII Ltd. presentation. June release.

CAST

T/Sgt. Jim Moore	Jack Webb
Pvt. Owens	Don Dubbins
Anne	Jackie Loughery
Capt. Anderson	Lin McCarthy
Burt	Monica Lewis
Mrs. Owens	Virginia Gregg
Hostess	Jeannie Beacham
Bartender	Lu Tobin
Guard	Earle Hodgins
Mother	Jeanne Baird
Customer	Barbara Pepper
Little Girl	Melody Gale

and Men of the U. S. Marine Corps

Left: Jack Webb, Jackie Loughery
Top: Jack Webb, Don Dubbins

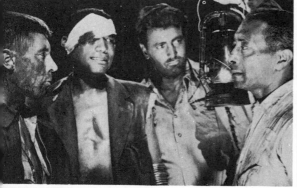

(M-G-M)
SOMETHING OF VALUE

Producer, Pandro S. Berman; Director, Richard Brooks; Screenplay by Richard Brooks; Based on Book by Robert C. Ruark; Music by Miklos Rozsa; Assistant Director, Joel Freeman; Wardrobe by Helen Rose. June release.

CAST

Peter McKenzie	Rock Hudson
Holly Keith	Dana Wynter
Elizabeth Newton	Wendy Hiller
Kimani	Sidney Poitier
Njogu	Juano Hernandez
Leader	William Marshall
Jeff Newton	Robert Beatty
Henry McKensie	Walter Fitzgerald
Joe Matson	Michael Pate
Lathela	Ivan Dixon
Karanja	Ken Renard
Witch Doctor	Samadu Jackson
Adam Marenga	Frederick O'Neal
Waithaka	John J. Akar

Wendy Hiller, Rock Hudson, Dana Wynter, Center: Michael Pate, Sidney Poitier, Rock Hudson, Juano Hernandez

Center: Sidney Poitier, Wendy Hiller

(M-G-M)

THE SEVENTH SIN

Producer, David Lewis; Director, Ronald Neame; Screenplay by Karl Tunberg; Based on Novel, "The Painted Veil," by Somerset Maugham; Music by Miklos Rozsa; Assistant Director, William McGarry; Wardrobe by Helen Rose; In CinemaScope. June release.

CAST

Carol Carwin	Eleanor Parker
Dr. Walter Carwin	Bill Travers
Tim Waddington	George Sanders
Paul Duvelle	Jean Pierre Aumont
Mother Superior	Francoise Rosay
Sister St. Joseph	Ellen Corby

Bill Travers, Eleanor Parker (also at top)

George Sanders, Ellen Corby, Eleanor Parker, Francoise Rosay
Top: Bill Travers, Jean Pierre Aumont, Eleanor Parker

(PARAMOUNT)

THE LONELY MAN

Producer, Pat Duggan; Director, Henry Levin; Screenplay by Harry Essex and Robert Smith; Music by Van Cleave; Song by Jack Brooks and Van Cleave; Sung by Tennessee Ernie Ford; Assistant Director, Bernard McEveety, Jr.; Filmed in VistaVision. June release.

CAST

Jacob Wade	Jack Palance
Riley Wade	Anthony Perkins
King Fisher	Neville Brand
Ben Ryerson	Robert Middleton
Ada Marshall	Elaine Aiken
Willie	Elisha Cook
Blackburn	Claude Akins
Faro	Lee Van Cleef
Dr. Fisher	Harry Shannon
Judge Hart	James Bell
Lon	Adam Williams
Sheriff	Denver Pyle
Sundown Whipple	John Doucette
Fence Green	Paul Newlan
Burnsey	Philip Van Zandt

and Moody Blanchard, Milton Frome, Tudor Owen, Russell Simpson, Taggert Casey, Daniel White, Richard Ryan, Billy Dix, Wesley Hudman, Zon Murry, Dirk London, Alan Page, Kenneth Hooker, Bill Meader.

Elaine Aiken, Anthony
Perkins

Anthony Perkins,
Robert Middleton

Jack Palance, Elaine Aiken,
Anthony Perkins

Anthony Perkins

Elaine Aiken, Jack Palance

Top: Anthony Perkins, Jack Palance

(UNITED ARTISTS)
SWEET SMELL OF SUCCESS

Producer, James Hill; Executive Producer, Harold Hecht; Screenplay by Clifford Odets and Ernest Lehman; Based on Novelette by Ernest Lehman; Director, Alexander Mackendrick; Music by Elmer Bernstein; Songs by Chico Hamilton and Fred Katz; A Norma-Curtleigh Production. June release.

CAST
J. J. Hunsecker	Burt Lancaster
Sidney Falco	Tony Curtis
Susan Hunsecker	Susan Harrison
Steve Dallas	Marty Milner
Frank D'Angelo	Sam Levene
Rita	Barbara Nichols
Sally	Jeff Donnell
Robard	Joseph Leon
Mary	Edith Atwater
Harry Kello	Emile Meyer
Herbie Temple	Joe Frisco
Otis Elwell	David White
Leo Bartha	Lawrence Dobkin
Mrs. Bartha	Lurene Tuttle
Mildred Tam	Queenie Smith
Linda	Autumn Russell
Manny Davis	Jay Adler
Al Evans	Lewis Charles

Tony Curtis, Burt
Lancaster

Susan Harrison, Sam
Levene, Marty Milner

Tony Curtis, Burt Lancaster
Top: Marty Milner, Tony Curtis, Burt
Lancaster, Susan Harrison, Sam Levene

Barbara Nichols, Tony Curtis
Top: Susan Harrison, Burt Lancaster

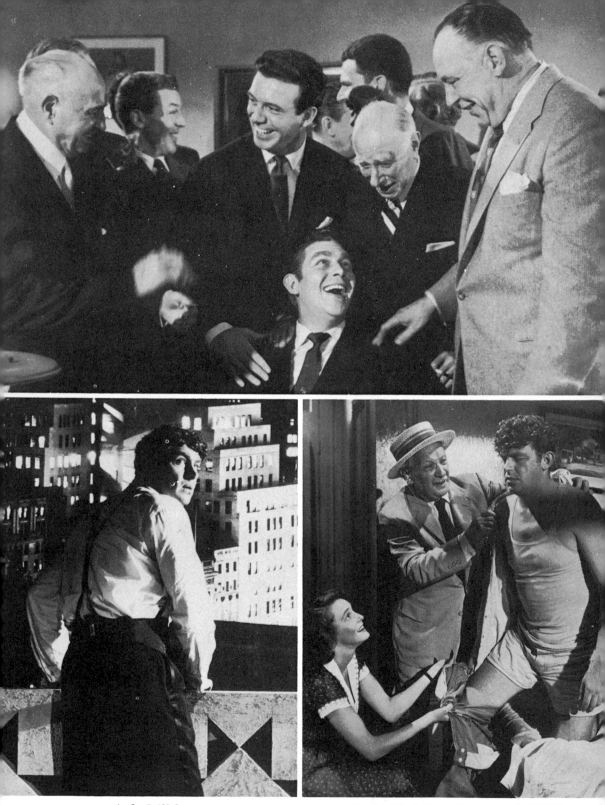

Andy Griffith   Patricia Neal, Percy Waram, Andy Griffith
Top: Percy Waram, Anthony Franciosa, Andy Griffith

(WARNER BROS.)

A FACE IN THE CROWD

A Newton Production; Director, Elia Kazan; Story and Screenplay by Budd Schulberg; Score by Tom Glazer; Songs by Tom Glazer and Budd Schulberg; Costumes by Anna Hill Johnstone; Wardrobe by Florence Transfield; Assistant Director, Charles H. Maguire. June release.

CAST

Lonesome Rhodes	Andy Griffith
Marcia Jeffries	Patricia Neal
Joey Kiely	Anthony Franciosa
Mel Miller	Walter Matthau
Betty Lou Fleckum	Lee Remick
Col. Hollister	Percy Waram
Beanie	Rod Brasfield
Mr. Luffler	Charles Irving
J. B. Jeffries	Howard Smith
Macey	Paul McGrath
1st Mrs. Rhodes	Kay Medford
Jim Collier	Alexander Kirkland
Senator Fuller	Marshall Nielan
Sheriff Hosmer	Big Jeff Bess
Abe Steiner	Henry Sharp

Andy Griffith, Patricia Neal (also at top)
Center: Walter Matthau, Patricia Neal

Center: Anthony Franciosa, Patricia Neal, Percy Waram

Parker Fennelly, Marjorie Main, John Smith,
Gloria Talbott, George Dunn

(UNIVERSAL)

THE KETTLES ON OLD MacDONALD'S FARM

Producer, Howard Christie; Director, Virgil Vogel; Screenplay by William Raynor and Herbert Margolis; Gowns by Marilyn Sotto; Assistant Director, Marshall Green. June Release.

CAST

Ma Kettle	Marjorie Main
Pa Kettle	Parker Fennelly
Sally Fleming	Gloria Talbott
Brad Johnson	John Smith
George	George Dunn
Pete Logan	Claude Akins
J. P. Flemming	Roy Barcroft
Bertha	Pat Morrow
Henry	George Arglen

Sal Mineo, Brian Keith

(ALLIED ARTISTS)

DINO

Producer, Bernice Block; Associate Producer, David Kramarsky; Director, Thomas Carr; Screenplay by Reginald Rose; Based on Teleplay by Reginald Rose; Assistant Director, Austen Jewell; Music by Gerald Fried; Wardrobe by Bert Henrickson. July release.

CAST

Dino	Sal Mineo
Sheridan	Brian Keith
Shirley	Susan Kohner
Mandel	Frank Faylen
Mr. Minetta	Joe DeSantis
Mrs. Minetta	Penny Santon
Tony	Pat DeSimone
Chuck	Richard Bakalyan
Frances	Mollie McCart
Sylvia	Cindy Robbins
Second Boy	Rafael Campos

Dick Beymer, Hal Stalmaster, Luana
Patten, Sharon Disney

(BUENA VISTA)

JOHNNY TREMAIN

Producer, Walt Disney; Director, Robert Stevenson; Screenplay by Tom Blackburn; Based on Novel by Esther Forbes; Music by George Bruns; Songs by George Bruns and Tom Blackburn; Assistant Director, William Beaudine, Jr.; Costumes, Chuck Keehne and Gertrude Casey; In Technicolor. July release.

CAST

Johnny Tremain	Hal Stalmaster
Cilla Lapham	Luana Patten
James Otis	Jeff York
Jonathan Lyte	Sebastian Cabot
Rab Silsbee	Dick Beymer
Paul Revere	Walter Sande
Samuel Adams	Rusty Lane
Josiah Quincy	Whit Bissell
Ephraim Lapham	Will Wright
Mrs. Lapham	Virginia Christine
Dr. Joseph Warren	Walter Coy
Major Pitcairn	Geoffrey Toone
General Gage	Ralph Clanton
Colonel Smith	Gavin Gordon
Admiral Montagu	Lumsden Hare
Jehu	Anthony Ghazlo, Jr.

Deborah Kerr

Cathleen Nesbitt, Cary Grant, Deborah Kerr

(20th CENTURY-FOX)

AN AFFAIR TO REMEMBER

Producer, Jerry Wald; Director, Leo McCarey; Screenplay by Delmer Daves and Leo McCarey; Story by Leo McCarey and Mildred Cram; Songs by Harry Warren and Harold Adamson and Leo McCarey; Music by Hugo Friedhofer; Sung by Vic Damone; Wardrobe Designer, Charles LeMaire; Assistant Director, Gilbert Mandelik; In CinemaScope and DeLuxe Color. July release.

CAST

Nickie Ferrante	Cary Grant
Terry McKay	Deborah Kerr
Kenneth	Richard Denning
Lois	Neva Patterson
Grandmother	Cathleen Nesbitt
Announcer	Robert Q. Lewis
Hathaway	Charles Watts
Courbet	Fortunio Bonanova
Father McGrath	Matt Moore
Mario	Louis Mercier
Miss Webb	Geraldine Wall
Gladys	Nora Marlowe
Miss Lane	Sarah Selby
Gabriello	Genevieve Aumont
Landlady	Jesslyn Fax
Bartender	Alberto Morin

Top: Cary Grant, Deborah Kerr
Left Center: Cary Grant, Minta Durfee, Deborah Kerr

Richard Denning, Deborah Kerr   Deborah Kerr, Cary Grant
Top: Louis Mercier, Deborah Kerr, Cathleen Nesbitt, Priscilla Garcia, Cary Grant

77

Martha Hyers, Jerry Lewis, Darren McGavin

(PARAMOUNT)

THE DELICATE DELINQUENT

Producer, Jerry Lewis; Written and Directed by Don McGuire; Assistant Director, Richard Caffey; Costumes by Edith Head; Assistant Producer, Jack Mintz; Music by Buddy Bregman; Musical Number Staged by Nick Castle; In VistaVision. July release.

CAST

Sidney Pythias	Jerry Lewis
Mike Damon	Darren McGavin
Martha	Martha Hyers
Monk	Robert Ivers
Captain Riley	Horace McMahon
Artie	Richard Bakalyan
Harry	Joseph Corey
Patricia	Mary Webster
Mr. Herman	Milton Frome
Mr. Crow	Jefferson Searles
Rocky Marciano	Himself
Sergeant Levitch	Emory Parnell
Kelly	Emile Meyer
Cadet Goerner	Dave Willock
Police Sergeant	Mike Ross

and Don Megowan, Irene Winston, Teru Shimada, Kazuo Togo, Don McGuire, Taggart Casey.

Top: Darren McGavin, Jerry Lewis
Left Center: Robert Ivers, Joseph Corey, Richard Bakalyan, Jerry Lewis

(UNIVERSAL)

JOE BUTTERFLY

Producer, Aaron Rosenberg; Director, Jesse Hibbs; Screenplay by Sy Gomberg, Jack Sher and Marion Hargrove; Based on a Play by Evan Wylie and Jack Ruge; Assistant Director, Phil Bowles; In CinemaScope and Technicolor. July release.

CAST

Joe Butterfly	Burgess Meredith
Pvt. John Woodley	Audie Murphy
Sgt. Ed Kennedy	George Nader
Henry Hathaway	Keenan Wynn
Cheiko	Keiko Shima
Col. E. E. Fuller	Fred Clark
Sgt. Dick Mason	John Agar
Sgt. Jim McNulty	Charles McGraw
Little Boy	Shinpei Shimazaki
False Tokyo Rose	Reiko Higa
Father	Tatsuo Saito
Mother	Chizu Shimazaki
Major Ferguson	Herbert Anderson
Sgt. Oscar Hulick	Eddie Firestone
Chief Yeoman Saul Bernheim	Frank Chase
Colonel Hopper	Herold Goodwin
Soldier	Willard Willingham

Top: George Nader, Keenan Wynn, Audie Murphy

Right Center: George Nader, Keenan Wynn, John Agar

Burgess Meredith, Audie Murphy

79

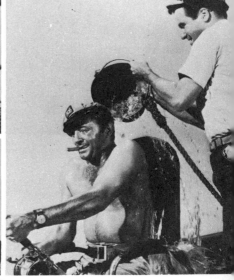

(COLUMBIA)

FIRE DOWN BELOW

Producers, Irving Allen and Albert R. Broccoli; Director, Robert Parrish; Associate Producer, Ronald Kinnoch; Music by Arthur Benjamin; Screenplay by Irwin Shaw; Based on Novel by Max Catto; Assistant Directors, Gus Agosti and Bluey Hill; Choreographer, Tutte Lemkow; Harmonica Theme by Jack Lemmon; Gowns by Balmain and Berman; In CinemaScope and Technicolor. July release.

CAST

Irena	Rita Hayworth
Felix	Robert Mitchum
Tony	Jack Lemmon
Harbor Master	Herbert Lom
Lt. Sellers	Bonar Colleano
Doctor Sam	Bernard Lee
Jimmy Jean	Edric Conner
Captain	Peter Illing
Mrs. Canaday	Joan Miller
Miguel	Anthony Newley
Hotel Owner	Eric Pohlmann
American	Lionel Murton
U. S. Sailors	Vivian Matalon, Gordon Tanner, Maurice Kaufmann
Bartender	Murray Kash
Waitress	Maya Koumani
Young Man	Phillip Baird
Drunken Young Man	Keith Banks

Rita Hayworth, Jack Lemmon
Top: Robert Mitchum, Bernard Lee, Jack Lemmon, Rita Hayworth
Center: Robert Mitchum, Jack Lemmon

Rita Hayworth

(PARAMOUNT)

BEAU JAMES

Producer, Jack Rose; Director, Melville Shavelson; Screenplay by Jack Rose and Melville Shavelson; Based on Book by Gene Fowler; Costumes by Edith Head; Assistant Director Michael D. Moore; Production Associate, Hal C. Kern; Narration by Walter Winchell; Dances and Musical Numbers Staged by Jack Baker; In VistaVision and Technicolor. July release.

CAST

Jimmy Walker	Bob Hope
Betty Compton	Vera Miles
Chris Nolan	Paul Douglas
Allie Walker	Alexis Smith
Charley Hand	Darren McGavin
Bernie Williams	Joe Mantell
Prosecutor	Horace McMahon
Dick Jackson	Richard Shannon
Arthur Julian	Willis Bouchey
Sid Nash	Sid Melton
George Jessel	Himself
Al Smith	Walter Catlett

Paul Douglas, Bob Hope
Top: Bob Hope, George Jessel

Bob Hope
Top: Alexis Smith, Bob Hope

(20th CENTURY-FOX)

BERNARDINE

Producer, Samuel G. Engel; Director, Henry Levin; Screenplay by Theodore Reeves; Based on Play by Mary Chase; Music by Lionel Newman; Assistant Director, Eli Dunn; Songs by Johnny Mercer, Nick Kenny, Charles Kenny, J. Fred Coots; Song Numbers Staged by Bill Foster; Wardrobe, Charles LeMaire; Costumes by Mary Wills; In CinemaScope and DeLuxe Color. July release.

CAST

Beau	Pat Boone
Jean	Terry Moore
Mrs. Wilson	Janet Gaynor
J. Fullerton Weldy	Dean Jagger
Sanford Wilson	Richard Sargent
Lt. Langley Beaumont	James Drury
Griner	Ronnie Burns
Mr. Beaumont	Walter Abel
Mrs. Beaumont	Natalie Schafer
Ruby	Isabel Jewell
Hilda	Edit Angold
Friedelhauser	Val Benedict
Cleo	Ernestine Wade
Mr. Mason	Russ Conway
Olson	Tom Pittman
Kinswood	Hooper Dunbar

Jack Costanzo and Orchestra.

Ronnie Burns, Russ Conway, Richard Sargent, Hooper Dunbar, Val Benedict, Pat Boone, Tom Pittman
Top: Val Benedict, Nancy Ratts

Dean Jagger, Janet Gaynor, Hooper Dunbar, Robert Malcolm
Top: Pat Boone

(UNITED ARTISTS)
THE PRIDE AND THE PASSION

Producer-Director, Stanley Kramer; Story and Screenplay by Edna and Edward Anhalt; Based on Novel, "The Gun," by C. S. Forester; Music by George Antheil; Assistant Director, Carter DeHaven, Jr.; Costumes, Joe King; Choreography, Paco Reyes; Song by Peggy Lee; In VistaVision and Technicolor. July release.

CAST

Capt. Anthony Trumbull	Cary Grant
Miguel	Frank Sinatra
Juana	Sophia Loren
General Jouvet	Theodore Bikel
Sermaine	John Wengraf
Ballinger	Jay Novello
Carlos	Jose Nieto
Jose	Carlos Larranaga
Vidal	Philip Van Zandt
Manolo	Paco el Laberinto

Frank Sinatra, Sophia Loren, Cary Grant

Top and Center: Sophia Loren, Frank Sinatra, Cary Grant

Mary Fickett, Malcolm Brodrick, Bing Crosby
Right: Malcolm Brodrick, Anne Seymour

Malcolm Brodrick, Bing Crosby

(M-G-M)

MAN ON FIRE

Producer, Sol C. Siegel; Director, Ranald MacDougall; Screenplay by Ranald MacDougall; Based on Story by Malvin Wald and Jack Jacobs. July release.

CAST

Earl Carleton................................Bing Crosby
Nina Wylie....................................Inger Stevens
Gwen Seward..............................Mary Fickett
Sam Dunstock.............................E. G. Marshall
Ted Carleton.............................Malcolm Brodrick
and Anne Seymour, Richard Eastham.

Center: Bing Crosby, Malcolm Brodrick, Mary Fickett, Richard Eastham, E. G. Marshall, Inger Stevens

(M-G-M)
THE LIVING IDOL

Producers, Albert Lewin and Gregorio Walerstein; Director, Albert Lewin; Story and Screenplay by Albert Lewin; Music by Manuel Esperon and Rudolfo Halffter; Costumes by Armando Valdes Peza and Ramon Valdiosera; Assistant Director, Jaime Contreras; Choreography by Jose Silva and David Campbell; Song by Ismael Diaz; Associate Mexican Director, Rene Cardona; In CinemaScope and Eastman Color. July release.

CAST

Terry Matthews	Steve Forrest
Juanita	Liliane Montevecchi
Dr. Alfred Stoner	James Robertson-Justice
Elena	Sara Garcia
Manuel	Eduardo Noriega

Left: Liliane Montevecchi, Steve Forrest, James Robertson Justice
Top: Liliane Montevecchi, Steve Forrest

Leslie Nielsen, Debbie Reynolds, Mildred Natwick
Center: (L) Leslie Nielsen, Debbie Reynolds
88 (R) Sidney Blackmer, Debbie Reynolds, Fay Wray

(UNIVERSAL)
TAMMY AND THE BACHELOR

Producer, Ross Hunter; Director, Joseph Pevney; Screenplay by Oscar Brodney; Based on Novel by Cid Ricketts Sumner; Gowns, Bill Thomas; Assistant Director, Joe Kenney; Music by Frank Skinner; Song by Jay Livingston and Ray Evans; Sung by The Ames Brothers; In CinemaScope and Technicolor. July release.

CAST

Tammy	Debbie Reynolds
Peter Brent	Leslie Nielsen
Grandpa	Walter Brennan
Barbara	Mala Powers
Professor Brent	Sidney Blackmer
Aunt Renie	Mildred Natwick
Mrs. Brent	Fay Wray
Alfred Bissle	Philip Ober
Ernie	Craig Hill
Osia	Louise Beavers
Tina	April Kent

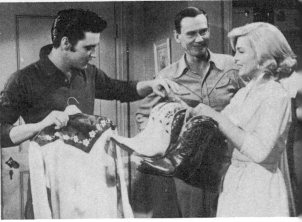

(PARAMOUNT)

LOVING YOU

Producer, Hal Wallis; Director, Hal Kanter; Screenplay by Herbert Baker and Hal Kanter; Story by Mary Agnes Thompson; Musical Numbers Staged by Charles O'Curran; Music by Walter Scharf; In VistaVision and Technicolor. August release.

CAST

Deke Rivers	Elvis Presley
Glenda Markle	Lizabeth Scott
Walker "Tex" Warner	Wendell Corey
Susan Jessup	Dolores Hart
Carl Meade	James Gleason
Skeeter	Paul Smith
Wayne	Ken Becker
Daisy	Jana Lund
Tallman	Ralph Dumke

Skip Young, Yvonne Lime and The Jordanaires

Ken Becker, Elvis Presley
Top: Dolores Hart, Elvis Presley, Lizabeth Scott

Center: Elvis Presley, Wendell Corey, Lizabeth Scott

89

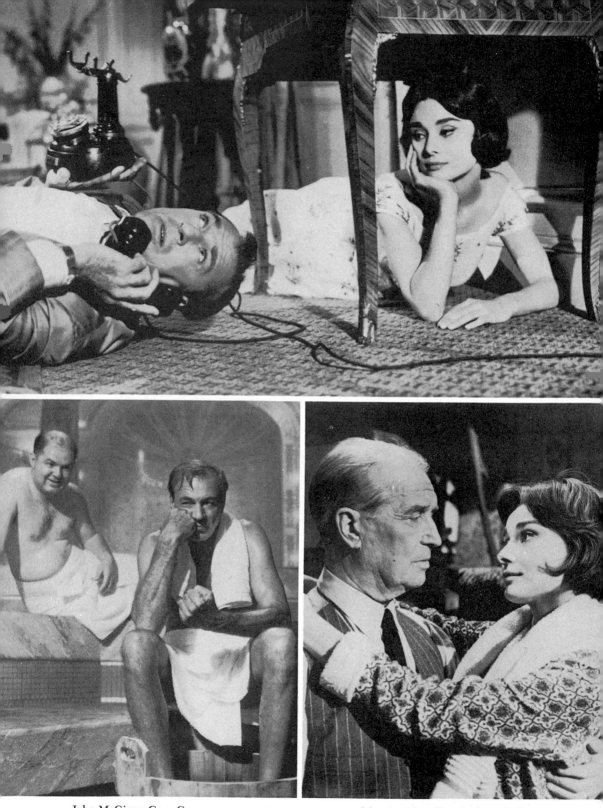

John McGiver, Gary Cooper

Maurice Chevalier, Audrey Hepburn

Top: Gary Cooper, Audrey Hepburn

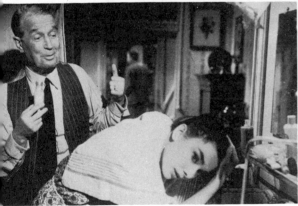

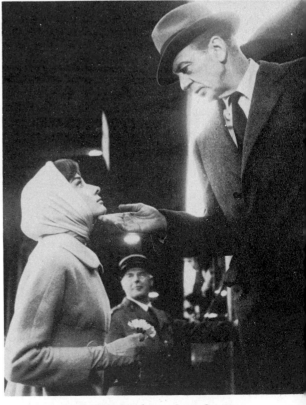

(ALLIED ARTISTS)

LOVE IN THE AFTERNOON

Producer-Director, Billy Wilder; Associate Producers, William Schorr and Doane Harrison; Screenplay by Billy Wilder and I. A. L. Diamond; Based on Novel by Claude Anet; Assistant Director, Paul Feyder; Music by F. D. Marchetti and Maurice de Feraudy, Henri Betti and Andre Hornez, Charles Trenet, Matty Malneck. July release.

CAST

Frank Flannagan	Gary Cooper
Ariane Chavasse	Audrey Hepburn
Claude Chavasse	Maurice Chevalier
Monsieur X	John McGiver
Michel	Van Doude
Madame X	Lise Bourdin
Woman Hotel Guest	Olga Valery
Gypsies	Matty Malneck, Gyula Kokas,
Michel Kokas, George Cicos, Victor Gazzoli	

Audrey Hepburn, Gary Cooper
Top: Gary Cooper, Audrey Hepburn

Center: Maurice Chevalier, Audrey Hepburn

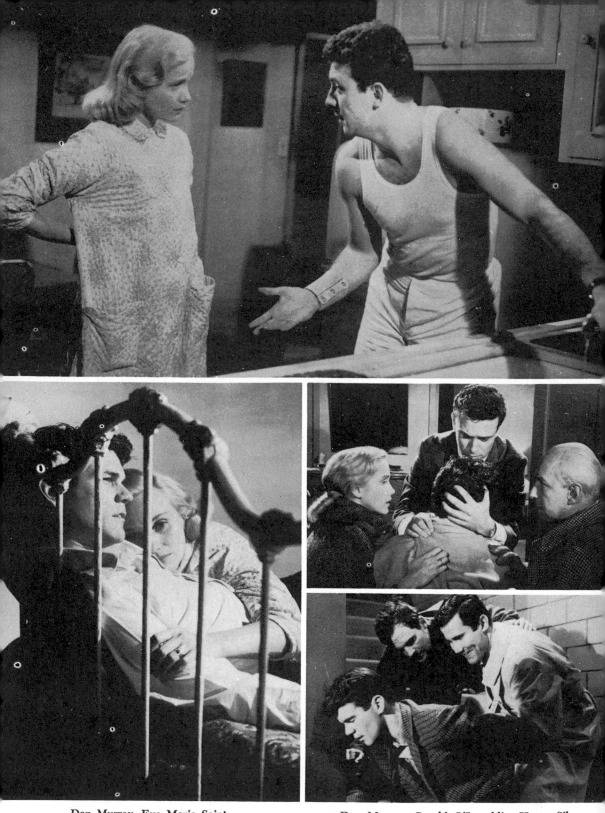

Don Murray, Eva Marie Saint
Top: Eva Marie Saint, Anthony Franciosa

Don Murray, Gerald O'Loughlin, Henry Silva
Center: Eva Marie Saint, Don Murray, Anthony Franciosa, Lloyd Nolan

(20th CENTURY-FOX)

A HATFUL OF RAIN

Producer, Buddy Adler; Director, Fred Zinnemann; Screenplay by Michael Vincente Gazzo and Alfred Hayes; Based on Play by Michael Vincente Gazzo; Music by Bernard Herrmann; Wardrobe by Charles LeMaire; Costumes by Mary Wills; Assistant Director, Ben Kadish; In CinemaScope. August release.

CAST

Celia Pope	Eva Marie Saint
Johnny Pope	Don Murray
Polo	Anthony Franciosa
John Pope, Sr	Lloyd Nolan
Mother	Henry Silva
Chuck	Gerald O'Loughlin
Apples	William Hickey

Eva Marie Saint, Don Murray

Don Murray, Anthony Franciosa

Top: Gerald O'Loughlin, Henry Silva, William Hickey, Anthony Franciosa, Don Murray

93

Gustavo Rojo, Martine Carol, Van Johnson

(M-G-M)

ACTION OF THE TIGER

Producer, Kenneth Harper; Director, Terence Young; Screenplay by Robert Carson; Based on Book by James Wellard; Adapted by Peter Myers; Associate Producer, George Willoughby; Executive Producers, Joseph Blau and Johnny Meyer; In CinemaScope and Technicolor. August release.

CAST

Carson	Van Johnson
Tracy	Martine Carol
Trifon	Herbert Lom
Henri	Gustavo Rojo
Security Officer	Tony Dawson
Mara	Anna Gerber
Katina	Yvonne Warren
The Countess	Helen Haye
Mike	Sean Connery
Kol Stendho	Pepe Nieto
Trifon's Father	Norman Macowan
Farmer's Wife	Helen Goss
Adbyll	Richard Williams

Anita Ekberg, Victor Mature

(COLUMBIA)

PICKUP ALLEY

Producers, Irving Allen, Albert R. Broccoli; Director, John Gilling; Screenplay by John Paxton; From a Story by A. J. Forrest; Wardrobe by Elsa Fennell; Assistant Director, Bluey Hill; A Warwick Production. August release.

CAST

Charles Sturgis	Victor Mature
Gina Borger	Anita Ekberg
Frank McNally	Trevor Howard
Amalio	Bonar Colleano
Salko	Alec Mango
Baris	Peter Illing
Jarolli	Martin Benson
Guido	Marne Maitland
Fayala	Eric Pohlmann
Drug Addict	Betty McDowall
Curtis	Sidney Tafler

and Gaylord Cavallaro, Lionel Murton, Harold Kasket, Peter Elliott. Alfredo Rizzo, Brian Wilde, Kevin Stoney, Umberto Fiz.

Cornel Wilde, Debra Paget

(PARAMOUNT)

OMAR KHAYYAM

Producer, Frank Freeman, Jr.; Director, William Dieterle; Screenplay by Barre Lyndon; Assistant Director, Francisco Day; Music by Victor Young; Costumes by Ralph Jester; Songs by Jay Livingston and Ray Evans, Mack David and Victor Young, and Moises Vivanco; In VistaVision and Technicolor. August release.

CAST

Omar	Cornel Wilde
Hassan	Michael Rennie
Sharain	Debra Paget
Malik	John Derek
The Shah	Raymond Massey
Karina	Yma Sumac
Zarada	Margaret Hayes
Yaffa	Joan Taylor
Prince Ahmud	Perry Lopez
Nizam	Sebastian Cabot
Imam Mowaffak	Morris Ankrum
Tutush	Abraham Sofaer
Jayhan	Edward Platt
Buzorg	James Griffith
Master Herald	Peter Adams
1st Commander	Henry Brandon
2nd Commander	Paul Picerni
Tutush Bodyguard	Kem Dibbs

James Dean, Second From Left

(WARNER BROS.)
THE JAMES DEAN STORY
Produced and Directed by George W. George and Robert Altman; Narration by Martin Gabel; Music by Leith Stevens; Theme Song by Jay Livingston and Ray Evans; Sung by Tommy Sands; Written by Stewart Stern. August release.

CAST
In Fairmount:

His Uncle	Marcus Winslow
His Aunt	Ortense Winslow
His Cousin	Markie Winslow
His Grandfather	Grandpa Dean
His Grandmother	Grandma Dean
His Dramatics Teacher	Adeline Nall
The Nurseryman	Bing Traster
Owner of Motorcycle Shop	Mr. Carter

In New York:

Owner of Bar	Jerry Luce
Waiter	Louie De Liso
Taxicab Driver	Arnie Langer
Girl in Apartment	Arline Sax
Girl At Actor's Studio	Chris White
Press Agent	George Ross

(M-G-M)
GUN GLORY
Producer, Nicholas Nayfack; Director, Roy Rowland; Screenplay by William Ludwig; Based on Novel, "Man Of The West," by Philip Yordan; Music by Jeff Alexander; Song sung by Burl Ives; Costumes by Walter Plunkett; Assistant Director, George Rhein; In CinemaScope and Metrocolor. August release.

CAST

Tom Early	Stewart Granger
Jo	Rhonda Fleming
Preacher	Chill Wills
Young Tom Early	Steve Rowland
Grimsell	James Gregory
Sam Wainscott	Jacques Aubuchon
Gunn	Arch Johnson

Rhonda Fleming, Steve Rowland,
Stewart Granger

(COLUMBIA)
THE YOUNG DON'T CRY
Producer, Philip A. Waxman; Director, Alfred L. Werker; Screenplay by Richard Jessup from his Novel; Music by George Antheil; Assistant Director, Sam Wurtzel. August release.

CAST

Leslie Henderson	Sal Mineo
Rudy Krist	James Whitmore
Plug	J. Carrol Naish
Max Cole	Gene Lyons
Bradley	Paul Carr
Clancy	Thomas Carlin
Doosy	Leigh Whipper
Billy	Stefan Gierasch
Whittaker	Victor Thorley
Maureen Cole	Roxanne
Mr. Gwinn	James Reese
Philomena	Ruth Attaway
Allan	Leland Mayforth
Jimmy	Dick Wigginton
Stanley	Stanley Martin
Mrs. Gwinn	Josephine Smith
Solomon	Joseph Killorin
Whigs	Phillips Hamilton
Hardhead	Victor Johnson

James Whitmore, Sal Mineo, Victor Thorley

(WARNER BROS.)
THE PAJAMA GAME

Produced and Directed by George Abbott and Stanley Donen; Associate Producers, Frederick Brisson, Robert E. Griffith and Harold S. Prince; Screenplay by George Abbott and Richard Bissell based on their play from Richard Bissell's Novel, "7½ Cents"; Music and Lyrics by Richard Adler and Jerry Ross; Choreography by Bob Fosse; Costumes by William and Jean Eckart assisted by Frank Thompson; Assistant Director, Russ Llewellyn; In WarnerColor. August release.

CAST

Babe	Doris Day
Sid	John Raitt
Gladys	Carol Haney
Hines	Eddie Foy, Jr.
Mabel	Reta Shaw
Poopsie	Barbara Nichols
Mae	Thelma Pelish
Prez	Jack Straw
Hasler	Ralph Dunn
Max	Owen Martin
Ist Helper	Jackie Kelk
Charlie	Ralph Chambers
Brenda	Mary Stanton
Featured Dancers	Buzz Miller, Kenneth LeRoy

John Raitt, Doris Day

Reta Shaw, Eddie Foy, Jr.
Top: Doris Day, John Raitt

Eddie Foy, Jr., Reta Shaw
Top: Carol Haney, Eddie Foy, Jr., Jack Waldron, John Raitt
Center: Doris Day, John Raitt, Carol Haney

Carol Haney

(UNIVERSAL)

THE MIDNIGHT STORY

Producer, Robert Arthur; Director, Joseph Pevney; Screenplay by John Robinson and Edwin Blum; Story by Edwin Blum; Gowns by Bill Thomas; Assistant Director, Joseph E. Kenny; In CinemaScope. August release.

CAST

Joe Martini	Tony Curtis
Anna Malatesta	Marisa Pavan
Sylvio Malatesta	Gilbert Roland
Sgt. Jack Gillen	Jay C. Flippen
Mama Malatesta	Argentina Brunetti
Lt. Kilrain	Ted de Corsia
Peanuts Malatesta	Richard Monda
Rosa Cuneo	Kathleen Freeman
Charlie Cuneo	Herbert Vigran
Veda Pinelli	Peggy June Maley
Father Giuseppe	John Cliff
Sgt. Sommers	Russ Conway
Frankie Pellatrini	Chico Vejar
Grocer	Tito Vuolo
Mother Catherine	Helen Wallace
Frank Wilkins	James Hyland

Left: Tony Curtis, Marisa Pavan, Argentina Brunetti, Gilbert Roland
Top: Tony Curtis, Peggy Maley

(20th CENTURY-FOX)

SEA WIFE

Producer, Andre Hakim; Associate Producer-Director, Paul Crosfield; Assistant Directors, Robert Lynn, Ted Sturgis, Jim Northcote; Wardrobe, Bill Walsh. August release.

CAST

Biscuit	Richard Burton
Seawife	Joan Collins
Bulldog	Basil Sydney
Number Four	Cy Grant
Teddy	Ronald Squire
Scribe	Joan Hickson
Mrs. Giass	Eileen Way

and Nora Nicholson, Edith Saville, John Wood, Harold Goodwin, Vilma Ann Leslie, Sandra Caron, Gibb McLaughlin, Roddy Hughes, Yvette Wyatt, M. Takagi, Otokichi Mkeda.

Center: Richard Burton, Joan Collins
Right Center: Richard Burton, Joan Collins, Basil Sydney

Gilbert Roland

Henry Jones, Barbara Eden, Tony Randall

Jayne Mansfield

Tony Randall,
Jayne Mansfield

Mickey Hargitay,
Tony Randall

Joan Blondell

(20th CENTURY-FOX)
WILL SUCCESS SPOIL ROCK HUNTER?

Producer-Director, Frank Tashlin; Story and Screenplay by Frank Tashlin; Based on Play by George Axelrod; Music by Cyril J. Mockridge; Wardrobe Designer, Charles LeMaire; Assistant Director, Joseph E. Rickards; Song by Bobby Troup; In CinemaScope and DeLuxe Color. August release.

CAST

Rita Marlowe	Jayne Mansfield
Rock Hunter	Tony Randall
Jenny	Betsy Drake
Violet	Joan Blondell
LaSalle, Jr.	John Williams
Rufus	Henry Jones
April	Lili Gentle
Bobo	Mickey Hargitay
Calypso Number	Georgia Carr
TV Interviewer	Dick Whittinghill
Gladys	Ann McCrea
Frenchmen	Alberto Morin, Louis Mercier

Mickey Hargitay,
Dick Whittinghill

(UNIVERSAL)

NIGHT PASSAGE

Producer, Aaron Rosenberg; Director, James Neilson; Screenplay by Borden Chase; Based on Story by Norman A. Fox; Costumes by Bill Thomas; Assistant Director, Marshall Green; Music by Dimitri Tiomkin; Songs by Ned Washington and Dimitri Tiomkin; In Technirama and Technicolor. August release.

CAST

Grant McLaine	James Stewart
The Utica Kid	Audie Murphy
Whitey Harbin	Dan Duryea
Charlotte Drew	Dianne Foster
Verna Kimball	Elaine Stewart
Joey Adams	Brandon de Wilde
Ben Kimball	Jay C. Flippen
Will Renner	Herbert Anderson
Concho	Robert J. Wilke
Jeff Kurth	Hugh Beaumont
Shotgun	Jack Elam
Howdy Sladen	Tommy Cook
Mr. Feeney	Paul Fix
Miss Vittles	Olive Carey
Tim Eiley	James Flavin
Jubilee	Donald Curtis
Mrs. Feeney	Ellen Corby

and John Day, Kenny Williams, Frank Chase, Herold Goodwin, Harold Tommy Hart, Jack C. Williams, Boyd Stockman, Henry Wills, Chuck Roberson, Willard Willingham, Polly Burson, Patsy Novak, Ted Mapes.

Left: Dianne Foster, Brandon De Wilde,
James Stewart, Audie Murphy
Top: Audie Murphy, Elaine Stewart

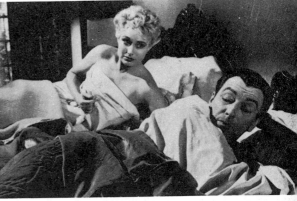

(M-G-M)

TIP ON A DEAD JOCKEY

Producer, Edwin H. Knopf; Director, Richard Thorpe; Screenplay by Charles Lederer; Based on Story by Irwin Shaw; Music by Miklos Rozsa; Song by Jerome Kern and P. G. Wodehouse; Assistant Director, William Shanks; Gowns by Helen Rose; In CinemaScope. August release.

CAST

Lloyd Tredman	Robert Taylor
Phyllis Tredman	Dorothy Malone
Paquita Heldon	Gia Scala
Bert Smith	Martin Gabel
Toto Del Aro	Marcel Dalio
Jimmy Heldon	Jack Lord
Sue Fan Finley	Joyce Jameson

Marcel Dalio, Martin Garralaga, Jack Lord,
Murphy, Gia Scala, Robert Taylor,
Dorothy Malone
Center: Jack Lord, Gia Scala, Marcel Dalio, Dorothy Malone, Robert Taylor

Clark Gable

Clark Gable, Larry Blake, Maurice Marsac, Yvonne De Carlo

Rex Reason, Yvonne De Carlo, Efrem Zimbalist, Jr.

(WARNER BROS.)

BAND OF ANGELS

Director, Raoul Walsh; Screenplay by John Twist, Ivan Goff and Ben Roberts; Based on Novel by Robert Penn Warren; Music by Max Steiner; Costumes by Marjorie Best; Assistant Directors, Russ Saunders and Al Alleborn; In WarnerColor. August release.

CAST

Hamish Bond	Clark Gable
Amantha Starr	Yvonne De Carlo
Rau-Ru	Sidney Poitier
Ethan Sears	Efrem Zimbalist, Jr.
Seth Parton	Rex Reason
Charles de Marigny	Patric Knowles
Capt. Canavan	Torin Thatcher
Miss Idell	Andrea King
Mr. Calloway	Ray Teal
Jimmee	Russ Evans
Michele	Carolle Drake
Stuart	Raymond Bailey
Dollie	Tommie Moore
Aaron Starr	William Forrest
Young Manty	Noreen Corcoran

Yvonne De Carlo, Clark Gable
Center: Yvonne De Carlo

Sidney Poitier, Clark Gable, William Schallert
Center: Clark Gable

105

(UNIVERSAL)

INTERLUDE

Producer, Ross Hunter; Director, Douglas Sirk; Screenplay by Daniel Fuchs and Franklin Coen; Adaption by Inez Cocke; Based on Screenplay by Dwight Taylor and a Story by James Cain; Gowns by Jay A. Morley, Jr., Assistant Director, Marshall Green; Music by Frank Skinner and Paul Francis Webster; Sung by the McGuire Sisters; In CinemaScope and Technicolor. September release.

CAST

Helen Banning	June Allyson
Toni Fischer	Rossano Brazzi
Reni Fischer	Marianne Cook
Countess Reinhart	Francoise Rosay
Dr. Morley Dwyer	Keith Andes
Gertrude	Frances Bergen
Housekeeper	Lisa Helwig
Henig	Herman Schwedt
Dr. Smith	Anthony Tripoli
Dr. Stein	John Stein
Prue Stubbins	Jane Wyatt

Marianne Cook, Gerd Klinkhardt, June Allyson
Center: (L) June Allyson, Keith Andes,
(R) Rossano Brazzi

106 Top: Rossano Brazzi, Francoise Rosay, Marianne Cook

(COLUMBIA)

3:10 TO YUMA

Producer, David Heilwell; Director, Delmer Daves; Screenplay by Halsted Welles; Based on Story by Elmore Leonard; Gowns by Jean Louis; Music by George Duning; Song by Ned Washington and George Duning; Sung by Frankie Laine; Assistant Director, Sam Nelson. September release.

CAST

Ben Wade	Glenn Ford
Dan Evans	Van Heflin
Emmy	Felicia Farr
Alice Evans	Leora Dana
Alex Potter	Henry Jones
Charlie Prince	Richard Jaeckel
Mr. Butterfield	Robert Emhardt
Bob Moons	Sheridan Comerate
Bartender	George Mitchell
Ernie Collins	Robert Ellenstein
Marshall	Ford Rainey
Mathew	Barry Curtis
Mark	Jerry Hartleben

Glenn Ford, Robert Emhardt, Van Heflin
Top: Van Heflin, Leora Dana, Glenn Ford
Center: (R) Glenn Ford, Richard Jaeckel,
(L) George Mitchell, Richard Jaeckel

RUN OF THE ARROW

An RKO Picture and Globe Enterprise Production; Written, Produced and Directed by Samuel Fuller; Assistant Director, Ben Chapman; Music by Victor Young; In Technicolor. September release.

CAST

O'Meara	Rod Steiger
Yellow Moccasin	Sarita Montiel
Capt. Clark	Brian Keith
Lt. Driscoll	Ralph Meeker
Walking Coyote	Jay C. Flippen
Blue Buffalo	Charles Bronson
Mrs. O'Meara	Olive Carey
Crazy Wolf	H. M. Wynant
Lt. Stockwell	Neyle Morrow
Red Cloud	Frank de Kova
General Allen	Col. Tim McCoy
Colonel Taylor	Stuart Randall
Ballad Singer	Frank Warner
Silent Tongue	Billy Miller
Corporal	Chuck Hayward
Sergeant	Chuck Roberson

Left: Rod Steiger, Ralph Meeker, Brian Keith
Top: Rod Steiger, Charles Bronson, Tim McCoy, Frank De Kova

HOUSE OF NUMBERS

Producer, Charles Schnee; Director, Russell Rouse; Associate Producer, James E. Newcom; Screenplay by Russell Rouse and Don Mankiewicz; Based on Novel by Jack Finney; Music by Andre Previn; Assistant Director, George Rhein; In CinemaScope. September release.

CAST

Bill Judlow	Jack Palance
Arnie Judlow	Jack Palance
Ruth Judlow	Barbara Lang
Henry Nova	Harold J. Stone
Warden	Edward Platt

Jack Palance in Dual Role

Jack Palance, Barbara Lang

John Wayne, Janet Leigh (also at top)
Center: (L) John Bishop, Jay C. Flippen, Richard
Rober, John Wayne, (R) John Wayne, Janet Leigh,
Paul Fix

(UNIVERSAL)

JET PILOT

Written and Produced by Jules Furthman;
Director, Josef von Sternberg; Assistant Director, Fred A. Fleck; Gowns by Michael
Woulfe; Music by Bronislau Kaper; An RKO
Production In Technicolor. September release.

CAST

Colonel Shannon	John Wayne
Anna	Janet Leigh
Major General Black	Jay C. Flippen
Major Rexford	Paul Fix
George Rivers	Richard Rober
Colonel Sokolov	Roland Winters
Colonel Matoff	Hans Conreid
General Langrad	Ivan Triesault
Major Sinclair	John Bishop
Georgia Rexford	Perdita Chandler
Mrs. Simpson	Joyce Compton
Mr. Simpson	Denver Pyle

and the United States Air Force

Tyrone Power, Mel Ferrer
Center: Robert Evans
Ava Gardner, Robert Evans
Center: Ava Gardner, Gregory Ratoff
Top: Ava Gardner, Tyrone Power, Robert Evans, Eddie Albert, Errol Flynn

(20th CENTURY-FOX)
THE SUN ALSO RISES

Producer, Darryl F. Zanuck; Director, Henry King; Screenplay by Peter Viertel; Based on Novel by Ernest Hemingway; Music by Hugo Friedhofer; In CinemaScope and DeLuxe Color. September release.

CAST

Jake Barnes	Tyrone Power
Lady Brett Ashley	Ava Gardner
Robert Cohn	Mel Ferrer
Mike Campbell	Errol Flynn
Bill Gorton	Eddie Albert
Count Mippipopolous	Gregory Ratoff
Georgette	Juliette Greco
Zizi	Marcel Dalio
Doctor	Henry Daniell
Harris	Bob Cunningham
The Girl	Danik Patisson
Romero	Robert Evans
Mr. Braddock	Eduardo Noriega
Mrs. Braddock	Jacqueline Evans
Montoya	Carlos Muzquiz
Frances	Rebecca Iturbi
Mgr. Romero	Carlos David Ortigos

Top: Robert Evans, Carlos Muzquiz, Tyrone Power, Eddie Albert
Center: Mel Ferrer, Ava Gardner, Tyrone Power

Tyrone Power (right)
Center: Tyrone Power, Ava Gardner

111

Natalie Trundy, Dean Stockwell

(UNITED ARTISTS)
THE CARELESS YEARS

Produced and Written by Edward Lewis; Director, Arthur Hiller; Music by Leith Stevens; Songs by Joe Lubin; Sung by Sue Raney; Assistant Director, John Burch; A Bryna Production. September release.

CAST

Jerry Vernon	Dean Stockwell
Emily Meredith	Natalie Trundy
Sam Vernon	John Larch
Helen Meredith	Barbara Billingsley
Charles Meredith	John Stephenson
Harriet	Maureen Cassidy
Bob Williams	Alan Dinehart III
Mathilda Vernon	Virginia Christine
Biff Vernon	Bobby Hyatt
Uncle Harry	Hugh Sanders
Aunt Martha	Claire Carleton
Mrs. Belosi	Lizz Slifer

Glenn Langan

(AMERICAN-INTERNATIONAL)
THE AMAZING COLOSSAL MAN

Producer-Director, Bert I. Gordon; Screenplay by Mark Hanna and Bert I. Gordon; Assistant Director, Nate D. Slott; Wardrobe by Bob Richards; Music by Albert Glasser; A Malibu Production. September release.

CAST

Lt. Col. Glenn Manning	Glenn Langan
Carol Forrest	Cathy Downs
Dr. Paul Lindstrom	William Hudson
Colonel Hallock	James Seay
Dr. Eric Coulter	Larry Thor
Richard Kingman	Russ Bender
Sgt. Taylor	Lynn Osborn
Typist	Diana Darrin
Control Officer	William Hughes
Henry	Hank Patterson
Sgt. Lee Carter	Scott Peters
Capt. Thomas	Myron Cook

and Jack Kosslyn, Jean Moorhead, Jimmy Cross, Frank Jenks, Harry Raybould, Michael Harris, Bill Cassady, Dick Nelson, Edmund Cobb, Judd Holdren, Paul Hahn, June Jocelyn, Stanley Lachman.

(COLUMBIA)
THE PARSON AND THE OUTLAW

Executive Producer, Robert Gilbert; Director, Oliver Drake; Assistant Director, Harry Webb; Music by Joe Sodja; Screenplay by Oliver Drake and John Mantley; A Charles "Buddy" Rogers Production in Technicolor. September release.

CAST

Billy The Kid	Anthony Dexter
Rev. Jericho Jones	Charles "Buddy" Rogers
Mrs. Jones	Jean Parker
Jack Slade	Sonny Tufts
Colonel Morgan	Robert Lowery
Tonya	Marie Windsor
Elly McCloud	Madalyn Trahey

and Bob Steel, Joe Sodja, Bob Duncan, Bob Gilbert, Jack Lowell, John Davis, Paul Spahn, Herman Pulver.

Jean Parker, Marie Windsor, Robert Lowery, Anthony Dexter, Madalyn Trahey, Sonny Tufts

(M-G-M)
THE HIRED GUN

Producers, Rory Calhoun and Victor M. Orsatti; Director, Ray Nazarro; Screenplay by David Lang and Buckley Angell; Music by Albert Glasser; Assistant Director, George Rhein; A Rorvic Production in CinemaScope. September release.

CAST

Gil McCord............................Rory Calhoun
Ellen Beldon..........................Anne Francis
Kell Beldon..........................Vince Edwards
Mace Beldon...............................John Litel
Judd Farrow........................Chuck Connors
Nathan Conroy.......................Robert Burton
Domingo Ortega..................Salvadore Baques
Elby Kirby........................Guinn Williams
Clint....................................Regis Parton

Anne Francis, Rory Calhoun

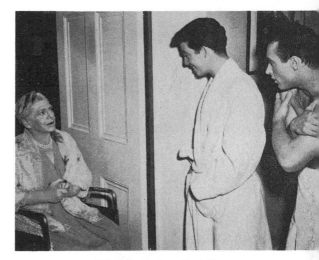

(WARNER BROS.)
JOHNNY TROUBLE

Producer-Director, John H. Auer; Executive Producer, John Carroll; Screenplay by Charles O'Neal and David Lord; Story by Ben Ames Williams; Music by Frank DeVol; Song by Peggy Lee; Sung by Eddie Robertson; Wardrobe by Rose Rockney; Assistant Director, Nate Barragar; A Clarion Production. September release.

CAST

Mrs. Chandler....................Ethel Barrymore
Tom McKay........................Cecil Kellaway
Julie..............................Carolyn Jones
Parsons................................Jesse White
Phil................................Rand Harper
Johnny............................Stuart Whitman
Eddie................................Jack Larson
Paul................................Paul Wallace
Elliott...........................Edward Byrnes
Tex.................................Joe Castagna
Charlie..............................Nino Tempo
Ike..................................Jim Bridges
Bill..............................Paul Lukather
Rev. Harrington.......................James Bell
Mr. Reichow........................Samuel Colt
Boy....................................Kip King
Madden................................Gavin Muir

Ethel Barrymore, Jack Larson,
Stuart Whitman

(UNIVERSAL)
THE UNHOLY WIFE

Producer-Director, John Farrow; Screenplay by Jonathan Latimer; From a Story by William Durkee; Assistant Director, Emmett Emerson; Gowns by Howard Shoup; Music by Daniele Amfitheatrof; An RKO Picture in Technicolor. October release.

CAST

Phyllis Hochen..........................Diana Dors
Paul Hochen..........................Rod Steiger
San....................................Tom Tryon
Emma Hochen........................Beulah Bondi
Gwen...............................Marie Windsor
Rev. Stephen Hochen..................Arthur Franz
Ezra Benton.......................Luis Van Rooten
Gino Verdugo.......................Joe De Santis
Theresa.........................Argentina Brunetti
Carl Kramer...........................Tol Avery
Sheriff Wattling....................James Burke
Deputy Watkins...................Steve Pendleton
Michael..............................Gary Hunley
Judge..........................Douglas Spencer

Rod Steiger, Diana Dors

(PARAMOUNT)
THE JOKER IS WILD

Producer, Samuel J. Briskin; Director, Charles Vidor; Screenplay by Oscar Saul; Based on Book by Art Cohn and Life of Joe E. Lewis; Assistant Director, C. C. Coleman, Jr.; Costumes by Edith Head; Dances staged by Josephine Earl; Songs by Sammy Cahn and James Van Heusen, and Harry Harris; In VistaVision. October release.

CAST

Joe E. Lewis	Frank Sinatra
Martha Stewart	Mitzi Gaynor
Letty Page	Jeanne Crain
Austin Mack	Eddie Albert
Cassie Mack	Beverly Garland
Swifty Morgan	Jackie Coogan
Capt. Hugh McCarthy	Barry Kelley
Georgie Parker	Ted de Corsia
Tim Coogan	Leonard Graves
Flora	Valerie Allen
Burlesque Comedian	Hank Henry
Mr. Page	Walter Woolf King

and Dennis McMullen, Wally Brown, Paul Salata, Bill Hickman, John Benson, Frank Mills, David Seigel, Robert Asquith, Larry Knight, Arturo Petterino, Harold Huber, Ned Glass, Ned (Edward) Wever, Don Beddoe, Mary Treen, Fred Catania, Sidney Melton, Paul Bryar, Dick Elliott, Billie Bird, John Harding, Ned LeFevre, Maurice Hart, Bill Baldwin, Ralph Montgomery, Billy Snyder, Joseph Donte, Paul Gary, Leon Martin, Russell Bender, Arthur Lewis, Lucy Knoch.

Top: Frank Sinatra, Eddie Albert, Beverly Garland

Frank Sinatra, Jeanne Crain
Top: Frank Sinatra

(UNITED ARTISTS)
TIME LIMIT!

Producers, Richard Widmark and William Reynolds; Directed by Karl Malden; Screenplay by Henry Denker; From the Play by Henry Denker and Ralph Berkey; Music by Fred Steiner; Assistant Director, Emmett Emerson; Wardrobe by Henry West; A Heath Production. October release.

CAST

Col. William Edwards	Richard Widmark
Major Harry Cargill	Richard Basehart
Cpl. Jean Evans	Dolores Michaels
Mrs. Cargill	June Lockhart
General Connors	Carl Benton Reid
Sgt. Baker	Martin Balsam
Lt. George Miller	Rip Torn
Mike	Alan Dexter
Capt. Joe Connors	Yale Wexler
Lt. Harvey	Manning Ross
Colonel Kim	Kaie Deei
Poleska	Skip McNally
Gus	Joe di Reda
Boxer	Kenneth Alton
Steve	James Douglas
Lt. Harper	Jack Webster

Top: James Douglas, Rip Torn, Yale Wexler, Joe DiReda
Right Center: Martin Balsam, Rip Torn, Richard Widmark

Richard Basehart, Carl Benton Reid, Richard Widmark

(20th CENTURY-FOX)
NO DOWN PAYMENT

Producer, Jerry Wald; Director, Martin Ritt; Screenplay by Philip Yordan; From the Novel by John McPartland; Music by Leigh Harline; Wardrobe, Charles LeMaire; Costumes, Mary Wills; Assistant Director, Eli Dunn; In Cinema-Scope. October release.

CAST

Leola Boone	Joanne Woodward
Isabelle Flagg	Sheree North
Jerry Flagg	Tony Randall
David Martin	Jeffrey Hunter
Troy Boone	Cameron Mitchell
Jean Martin	Patricia Owens
Betty Kreitzer	Barbara Rush
Herman Kreitzer	Pat Hingle
Markham	Robert Harris
Iko	Aki Aleong
Mr. Burton	Jim Hayward
Sandra Kreitzer	Mimi Gibson
Harmon Kreitzer	Donald Towers
Michael Flagg	Charles Herbert

Left: Cameron Mitchell, Pat Hingle, Jeffrey Hunter

Top: Sheree North, Tony Randall, Barbara Rush, Pat Hingle, Cameron Mitchell, Joanne Woodward, Jeffrey Hunter, Patricia Owens

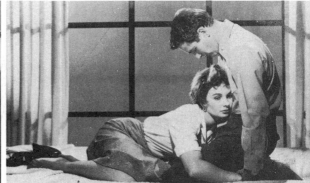

(M-G-M)
UNTIL THEY SAIL

Producer, Charles Schnee; Director, Robert Wise; Screenplay by Robert Anderson; Based on Story by James A. Michener; Associate Producer, James E. Newcom; Music by David Raksin; Song by David Raksin and Sammy Cahn; Sung by Eydie Gorme; Assistant Director, Ridgeway Callow; In CinemaScope. October release.

CAST

Barbara Leslie Forbes	Jean Simmons
Anne Leslie	Joan Fontaine
Capt. Jack Harding	Paul Newman
Delia Leslie	Piper Laurie
Capt. Richard Bates	Charles Drake
Evelyn Leslie	Sandra Dee
"Shinner" Phil Friskett	Wally Cassell
Prosecution	Alan Napier
Max Murphy	Ralph Votrian
Tommy	John Wilder
Marine	Tige Andrews
Lt. Andy	Adam Kennedy
Marine	Mickey Shaughnessy

Charles Drake, Sandra Dee, Joan Fontaine, Jean Simmons
Center: Jean Simmons, Piper Laurie, Adam Kennedy

Center: Jean Simmons, Paul Newman

116

(COLUMBIA)

THE STORY OF
ESTHER COSTELLO

Producer, Jack Clayton; Director, David Miller; Screenplay by Charles Kaufman; From the Novel by Nicholas Monsarrat; Gowns by Jean Louis; Assistant Directors, Peter Bolton and Roger Good; Music by Georges Auric; A Romulus Film. October reelase.

CAST

Margaret Landi	Joan Crawford
Carlo Landi	Rossano Brazzi
Esther Costello	Heather Sears
Harry Grant	Lee Patterson
Wenzel	Ron Randell
Mother Superior	Fay Compton
Paul Marchant	John Loder
Father Devlin	Denis O'Dea
Ryan	Sidney James
Matron in Art Gallery	Bessie Love
Mr. Wilson	Robert Ayres
Jennie Costello	Maureen Delaney
Tammy	Estelle Brody
Mrs. Forbes	June Clyde
Susan North	Sally Smith
Nurse Evans	Megs Jenkins
Dr. Stein	Andrew Cruickshank

and Harry Hutchinson, Tony Quinn, Janina Faye, Diana Day, Victor Rietti, Sheila Manahan.

Top: (L) Heather Sears, Joan Crawford, Rossano Brazzi, Ron Randell, (R) Rossano Brazzi, Joan Crawford

Center: (L) Lee Patterson, Joan Crawford, Heather Sears, John Loder, (R) Heather Sears, Denis O'Dea, Joan Crawford

Heather Sears, Lee Patterson
Above: Bessie Love, Rossano Brazzi, Joan Crawford

117

James Cagney
Top: Dorothy Malone, James Cagney

Marjorie Rambeau, James Cagney
Center: Roger Smith, James Cagney

(UNIVERSAL)
MAN OF A THOUSAND FACES

Producer, Robert Arthur; Director, Joseph Pevney; Screenplay by R. Wright Campbell, Ivan Goff and Ben Roberts; Story by Ralph Wheelwright; Costumes by Bill Thomas; Assistant Director, Phil Bowles; Music by Frank Skinner; In CinemaScope. October release.

CAST

Lon Chaney	James Cagney
Cleva Creighton Chaney	Dorothy Malone
Hazel Bennet	Jane Greer
Gert	Marjorie Rambeau
Clarence Locan	Jim Backus
Irving Thalberg	Robert J. Evans
Mrs. Chaney	Celia Lovsky
Carrie Chaney	Jeanne Cagney
Dr. J. Wilson Shields	Jack Albertson
Creighton Chaney at 21	Roger Smith
13	Robert Lyden
8	Rickie Sorensen
4	Dennis Rush
Pa Chaney	Nolan Leary
Carl Hastings	Simon Scott
Clarence Kolb	Himself
Max Dill	Danny Beck
George Loane Tucker	Phil Van Zandt
Comedy Waiters	Hank Mann, Snub Pollard

James Cagney

James Cagney

Center: Clarence Kolb, James Cagney, Danny Beck

119

Walter Winchell, Ann Blyth,
Cara Williams

Ann Blyth, Paul Newman

Richard Carlson,
Ann Blyth

(WARNER BROS.)

THE HELEN MORGAN STORY

Producer, Martin Rackin; Director, Michael Curtiz; Screenplay by Oscar Saul, Dean Reisner, Stephen Longstreet and Nelson Gidding; Musical Numbers Staged by LeRoy Prinz; Songs Sung by Gogi Grant; Costumes by Howard Shoup; Assistant Director, Paul Helmick; In CinemaScope. October release.

CAST

Helen	Ann Blyth
Larry	Paul Newman
Wade	Richard Carlson
Whitey Krause	Gene Evans
Ben	Alan King
Dolly	Cara Williams
Sue	Virginia Vincent
Ziegfeld	Walter Woolf King
Mrs. Wade	Dorothy Green
Haggerty	Ed Platt
Hellinger	Warren Douglas
Sammy	Sammy White

and The DeCastro Sisters, Jimmy McHugh, Rudy Vallee, Walter Winchell.

Paul Newman,
Ann Blyth

Jimmy McHugh, Walter Woolf King, Ann
Blyth, Richard Carlson, Maurice Marsac

Ann Blyth

Ann Blyth

(20th CENTURY-FOX)
THE THREE FACES OF EVE

Produced, Directed and Screenplay by Nunnally Johnson; Based on Book by Corbett H. Thigpen and Hervey M. Cleckley; Narration by Allistair Cooke; Music by Robert Emmett Dolan; Wardrobe, Charles LeMaire; Costumes by Renie; Assistant Director, David Hall; In CinemaScope. October release.

CAST

Eve	Joanne Woodward
Ralph White	David Wayne
Dr. Luther	Lee J. Cobb
Dr. Day	Edwin Jerome
Secretary	Alena Murray
Mrs. Black	Nancy Kulp
Mr. Black	Douglas Spencer
Bonnie	Terry Ann Ross
Earl	Ken Scott
Eve at 8	Mimi Gibson

Joanne Woodward
Top: Lee J. Cobb, Joanne
Woodward, Edwin Jerome

122

Center: David Wayne, Joanne Woodward

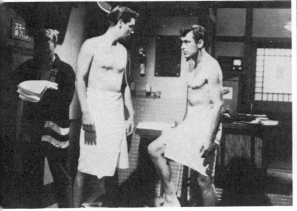

(20th CENTURY-FOX)
STOPOVER TOKYO

Producer, Walter Reisch; Director, Richard L. Breen; Screenplay by Richard L. Breen and Walter Reisch; Based on Novel by John P. Marquand; Music by Paul Sawtell; Assistant Director, Joseph E. Rickards; Wardrobe, Charles LeMaire; In CinemaScope and DeLuxe Color. November release.

CAST

Mark Fannon	Robert Wagner
Tina	Joan Collins
George Underwood	Edmond O'Brien
Tony Barrett	Ken Scott
Koko	Reiko Oyama
High Commissioner	Larry Keating
Wife of High Commissioner	Sarah Selby
Nobika	Solly Nakamura
Katsura	K. J. Seijto
Lt. Afumi	H. Okhawa

Top: Ken Scott, Robert Wagner, Joan Collins
Center: Robert Wagner, Ken Scott

Joan Collins, Robert Wagner
Center: Robert Wagner, Edmond O'Brien　123

(UNIVERSAL)

SLAUGHTER ON
TENTH AVENUE

Producer, Albert Zugsmith; Director, Arnold
Laven; Screenplay by Lawrence Roman; Based
on "The Man Who Rocked The Boat" by
William J. Keating and Richard Carter; Gowns
by Bill Thomas; Assistant Director, Phil
Bowles; Song by Richard Rodgers. November
release.

CAST

William Keating	Richard Egan
Madge Pitts	Jan Sterling
John Jacob Masters	Dan Duryea
Dee	Julie Adams
Al Dahlke	Walter Matthau
Lt. Anthony Vosnick	Charles McGraw
Howard Rysdale	Sam Levene
Solly Pitts	Mickey Shaughnessy
Benjy Karp	Harry Bellaver
Midget	Nick Dennis
Eddie "Cockeye" Cook	Ned Weaver
"Monk" Mohler	Billy M. Greene
Judge	John McNamara
Mrs. Cavanagh	Amzie Strickland
Big John	Mickey Hargitay

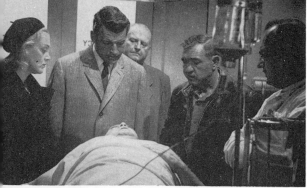

Left: Jan Sterling, Richard Egan, Joe Greene,
Harry Bellaver, George Becwar,
Mickey Shaughnessy (on table)

Top: Richard Egan, Julie Adams,
Charles McGraw

(WARNER BROS.)

BOMBERS B-52

Producer, Richard Whorf; Director, Gordon
Douglas; Screenplay by Irving Wallace; Story
by Sam Rolfe; Music by Leonard Rosenman;
Costumes by Howard Shoup; Assistant Direc-
tor, William Kissel; In CinemaScope and
WarnerColor. November release.

CAST

Lois Brennan	Natalie Wood
Sgt. Chuck Brennan	Karl Malden
Edith Brennan	Marsha Hunt
Col. Jim Herlihy	Efrem Zimbalist, Jr.
Sgt. Darren McKine	Don Kelly
Gen. Wayne Acton	Nelson Leigh
Stuart	Robert Nichols
Barnes	Ray Montgomery
Simpson	Bob Hover

Karl Malden, Natalie Wood

Center: Natalie Wood, Efrem Zimbalist, Jr.

(PARAMOUNT)
ZERO HOUR!

Producer, John C. Champion; Director, Hall Bartlett; Screenplay by Arthur Hailey, Hall Bartlett and John C. Champion; Story by Arthur Hailey; Music by Ted Dale; Songs by Arthur Hamilton, Billy Regis; Played by Billy Regis Band; Wardrobe by Eddie Armand Scheffer; Assistant Director, Lee Lukather. November release.

CAST

Ted Stryker	Dana Andrews
Ellen Stryker	Linda Darnell
Treleaven	Sterling Hayden
Captain Wilson	Elroy "Crazylegs" Hirsch
Dr. Baird	Geoffrey Toone
Tony Decker	Jerry Paris
Stewardess	Peggy King
Mrs. Wilson	Carole Eden
Burdick	Charles Quinlivan
Joey Stryker	Raymond Ferrell
Whitmond	David Thursby
Flight Dispatcher	Russell Thorson
Baby Sitter	Joanne Wade
Station Manager	Richard Keith
Co-Pilot Stewart	Steve London
TV Singer	John Ashley
RCAF Doctor	Willis Bouchey

and Maxine Cooper, David Thursby, Noel Drayton, Fintan Meyler, Larry Thor, Robert Stevenson, Mary Newton, Will Sage, Will White, Hope Summers, Arthur Hanson, Roy Gordon.

Left: Peggy King, Geoffrey Toone, Elroy Hirsch

Top: Russell Thorson, Sterling Hayden, Carole Eden

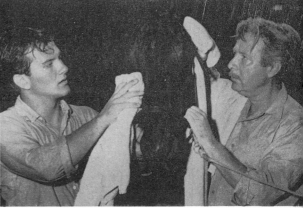

(20th CENTURY-FOX)
APRIL LOVE

Producer, David Weisbart; Director, Henry Levin; Screenplay by Winston Miller; Based on Novel by George Agnew Chamberlain; Songs by Paul Francis Webster and Sammy Fain; Assistant Director, Stanley Hough; Wardrobe, Charles LeMaire; Costumes by Renie; Musical Numbers Staged by Bill Foster; In CinemaScope and DeLuxe Color. November release.

CAST

Nick Conover	Pat Boone
Liz Templeton	Shirley Jones
Fran	Dolores Michael
Jed	Arthur O'Connell
Dan Templeton	Mat Crowley
Henrietta	Jeanette Nolan
Al Turner	Brad Jackson

Pat Boone, Shirley Jones

Center: Pat Boone, Arthur O'Connell

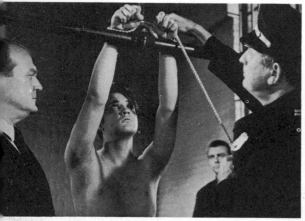

(M-G-M)

JAILHOUSE ROCK

Producer, Pandro S. Berman; Director, Richard Thorpe; Associate Producer, Kathryn Hereford; Screenplay by Guy Trosper; Based on Story by Ned Young; Songs by Mike Stoller and Jerry Leiber, and Roy C. Bennett, Aaron Schroeder, Abner Silver, Sid Tepper, Ben Weisman; Assistant Director, Robert E. Relyea; An Avon Production in CinemaScope.

CAST

Vince Everett	Elvis Presley
Peggy Van Alden	Judy Tyler
Hunk Houghton	Mickey Shaughnessy
Mr. Shores	Vaughn Taylor
Sherry Wilson	Jennifer Holden
Teddy Talbot	Dean Jones
Laury Jackson	Anne Neyland

Jennifer Holden, Elvis Presley
Top: William Forrest, Jennifer Holden, Elvis Presley

Elvis Presley (also at top)
Center: Judy Tyler, Elvis Presley

Anthony Quinn

(ALLIED ARTISTS)

THE HUNCHBACK OF NOTRE DAME

Producers, Robert and Raymond Hakim; Director, Jean Delannoy; Assistant Directors. Pierre Zimmer and Alain Kaminker; Music and Songs by Georges Auric, Angelo Lavagnino and Paul Lafargs; Costumes by Colosantis and Benda; A Paris Film Production in CinemaScope and Technicolor. November release.

CAST

Esmeralda	Gina Lollobrigida
Ouasimodo	Anthony Quinn
Phoebus	Jean Danet
Claude Frollo	Alain Cuny
Clopin Trouillefou	Philippi Clay
Fleur De Lys	Danielle Dumont
Gringoire	Robert Hirsch
Mathis Hungadi	Roger Blin
La Falourdel	Marianne Oswald
Louis XI	Jean Tissier
Guillaume Rousseau	Duphilo
Le Nabot	Pieral
Charmolue	Jacques Hilling
Jehan Frollo	Maurice Sarfati

Top: (L) Alain Cuny, Anthony Quinn
(R) Gina Lollobrigida, Anthony Quinn
Center (L) Anthony Quinn, (R) Gina
Lollobrigida, Anthony Quinn

127

Kay Kendall
Top: Gene Kelly, Taina Elg, Kay Kendall, Mitzi Gaynor

Kay Kendall, Taina Elg, Mitzi Gaynor, Gene Kelly
Center: Kay Kendall, Taina Elg, Mitzi Gaynor

(M-G-M)

LES GIRLS

Producer, Sol C. Siegel; Associate Producer, Saul Chaplin; Director, George Cukor; Screenplay by John Patrick; Story by Vera Gaspary; Music and Lyrics by Cole Porter; Choreography by Jack Cole; In CinemaScope and Metrocolor. November release.

CAST

Barry Nichols	Gene Kelly
Joy Henderson	Mitzi Gaynor
Lady Wren	Kay Kendall
Angele Ducros	Taina Elg
Pierre Ducros	Jacques Bergerac
Sir Gerald Wren	Leslie Phillips
Judge	Henry Daniell
Sir Percy	Patrick MacNee
Mr. Outward	Stephen Vercoe
Associate Judge	Philip Tonge

Jacques Bergerac, Gene Kelly, Leslie Phillips
Top: Gene Kelly, Kay Kendall

Jacques Bergerac, Taina Elg, Kay Kendall
Top: Taina Elg, Mitzi Gaynor, Kay Kendall, Gene Kelly

(COLUMBIA)
OPERATION MAD BALL

Producer, Jed Harris; Director, Richard Quine; Screenplay by Arthur Carter, Jed Harris, Blake Edwards; From a Play by Arthur Carter; Music by George Duning; Song by Fred Karger and Richard Quine; Assistant Director, Carter DeHaven, Jr. November release.

CAST

Pvt. Hogan	Jack Lemmon
Lt. Betty Bixby	Kathryn Grant
Capt. Paul Lock	Ernie Kovacs
Col. Rousch	Arthur O'Connell
Yancey Skibo	Mickey Rooney
Cpl. Bohun	Dick York
Pvt. Widowskas	James Darren
Cpl. Berryman	Roger Smith
Pvt. Grimes	William Leslie
Sgt. Wilson	Sheridan Comerate
Ozark	L. Q. Jones
Madame LaFour	Jeanne Manet
Lt. Johnson	Bebe Allen
Lt. Schmidt	Mary LaRoche
Sgt. McCloskey	Dick Crockett
Pvt. Bullard	Paul Picerni
Master Sgt. Pringle	David McMahon

Top: Paul Picerni, Dick York, Dick Crockett, James Darren, William Hickey, William Leslie, L. Q. Jones, Joel Collin, Jack Lemmon, Roger Smith
Right Center: Dick York, Mickey Rooney, Jack Lemmon

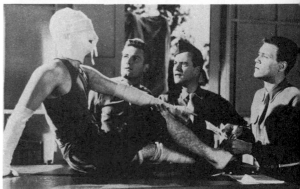

Kort Falkenberg, William Leslie, Jack Lemmon, Roger Smith

(PARAMOUNT)

THE TIN STAR

Producers, William Perlberg and George Seaton; Director, Anthony Mann; Screenplay by Dudley Nichols; Story by Barney Slater and Joel Kane; Assistant Director, Michael D. Moore; Costumes by Edith Head; Music by Elmer Bernstein; In VistaVision. November release.

CAST

Morg Hickman	Henry Fonda
Ben Owens	Anthony Perkins
Nona Mayfield	Betsy Palmer
Kip Mayfield	Michel Ray
Bogardus	Neville Brand
Dr. McCord	John McIntire
Millie	Mary Webster
Zeke McGaffey	Peter Baldwin
Buck Henderson	Richard Shannon
Ed McGaffey	Lee Van Cleef
Judge Thatcher	James Bell
Harvey King	Howard Petrie
Clem Hall	Russell Simpson
Andy Miller	Hal K. Dawson
Sam Hodges	Jack Kenney
McCall	Mickey Finn

and Frank Cady, Bob Kenaston, Allen Gettel, Frank Cordell, Frank McGrath, Tim Sullivan.

Michel Ray, Betsy Palmer

Top: (L) Anthony Perkins, (R) Anthony Perkins,
Henry Fonda
Left Center: Neville Brand, Henry Fonda,
Anthony Perkins

Perri

(BUENA VISTA)

PERRI

Presented by Walt Disney; Produced and Narrated by Winston Hibler; Directed by N. Paul Kenworthy, Jr., and Ralph Wright; Written by Ralph Wright and Winston Hibler; Based on Novel by Felix Salten; Music by Paul Smith; Songs by George Bruns, Paul Smith, Gil George, Ralph Wright, Winston Hibler; A true-life fantasy in Technicolor. November release.

Jon Provost, Roger Nakagawa

(UNIVERSAL)

ESCAPADE IN JAPAN

Producer-Director, Arthur Lubin; Written by Associate Producer Winston Miller; Assistant Director, Gordon McLean; Music by Max Steiner; An RKO Picture in Technirama and Technicolor. November release.

CAST

Mary Saunders	Teresa Wright
Dick Saunders	Cameron Mitchell
Tony Saunders	Jon Provost
Hiko	Roger Nakagawa
Lt. Col. Hargrave	Philip Ober
Michiko	Kuniko Miyake
Kei Tanaka	Susumu Fujita
Capt. Hibino	Katsuhiko Haida
Mr. Fushimi	Tatsuo Saito
Dekko-San	Hideko Koshikawa
Chief of Koyoto Police	Ureo Egawa
Farmer	Frank Tokunaga
Farmer's Wife	Ayako Hidaka

Mickey Rooney, Carolyn Jones

(UNITED ARTISTS)

BABY FACE NELSON

Producer, Al Zimbalist; Director, Don Siegel; Screenplay by Irving Shulman and Daniel Mainwaring; Story by Irving Shulman; Associate Producer, Byron Roberts; Assistant Director, J. Greenwald; A Fryman-Zs Production. November release.

CAST

Nelson	Mickey Rooney
Sue	Carolyn Jones
Doc Saunders	Cedric Hardwicke
Jerry	Chris Dark
Rocca	Ted DiCorsia
Mac	Emile Meyer
Hamilton	Tony Caruso
Dillinger	Leo Gordon
Miller	Dan Terranova
Fatso	Jack Elam
Bonner	Dabbs Greer
Johnson	Bob Osterloh
Powell	Dick Crockett
Aldridge	Paul Baxley
Connelly	Thayer David
Van Meter	Elisha Cook

and Ken Patterson, Sol Gorse, Gil Perkins, Tom Fadden, Lisa Davis, John Hoyt, Murray Alper, George Stone, Hubie Kerns

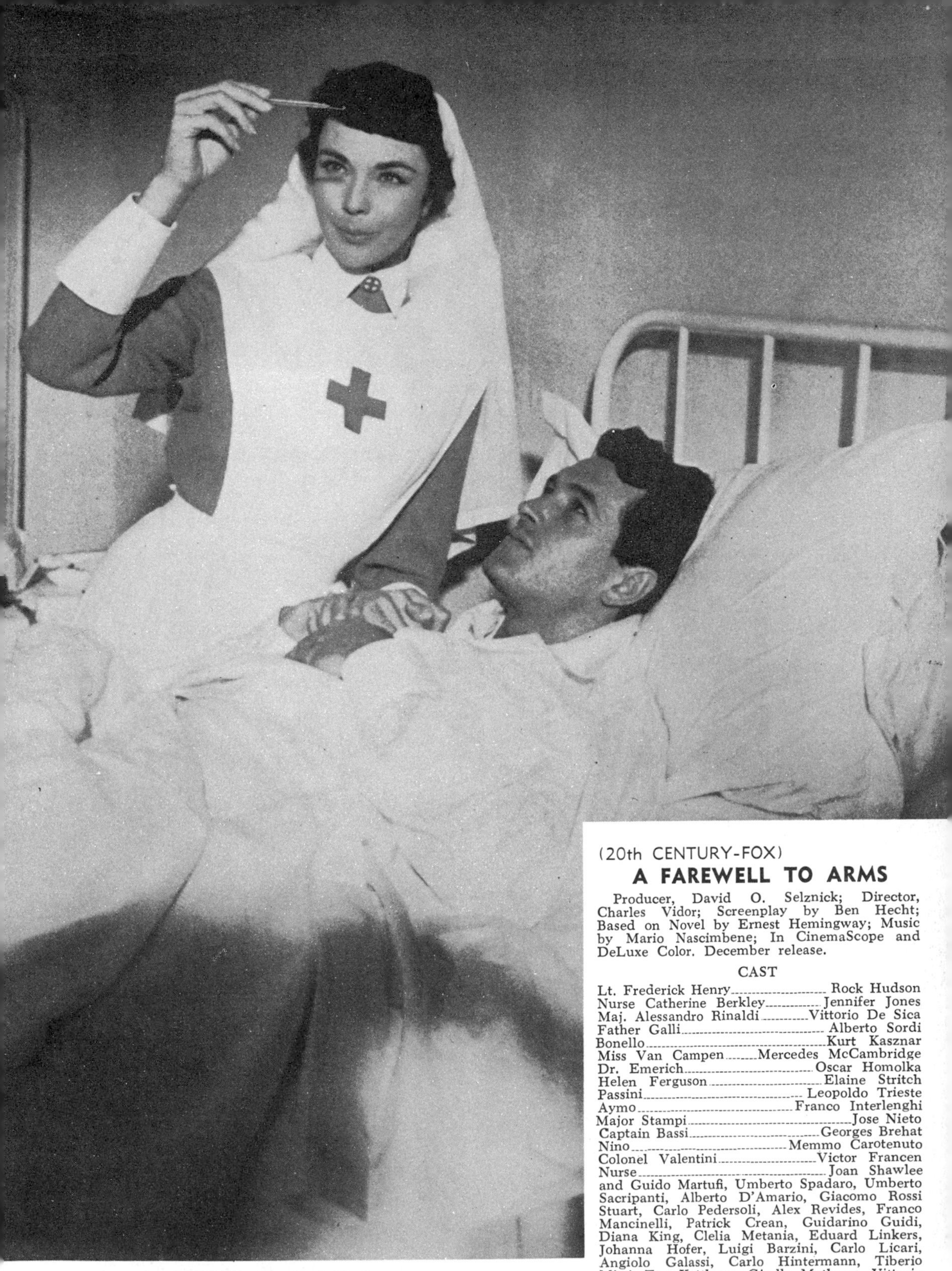

Jennifer Jones, Rock Hudson

(20th CENTURY-FOX)

A FAREWELL TO ARMS

Producer, David O. Selznick; Director, Charles Vidor; Screenplay by Ben Hecht; Based on Novel by Ernest Hemingway; Music by Mario Nascimbene; In CinemaScope and DeLuxe Color. December release.

CAST

Lt. Frederick Henry	Rock Hudson
Nurse Catherine Berkley	Jennifer Jones
Maj. Alessandro Rinaldi	Vittorio De Sica
Father Galli	Alberto Sordi
Bonello	Kurt Kasznar
Miss Van Campen	Mercedes McCambridge
Dr. Emerich	Oscar Homolka
Helen Ferguson	Elaine Stritch
Passini	Leopoldo Trieste
Aymo	Franco Interlenghi
Major Stampi	Jose Nieto
Captain Bassi	Georges Brehat
Nino	Memmo Carotenuto
Colonel Valentini	Victor Francen
Nurse	Joan Shawlee

and Guido Martufi, Umberto Spadaro, Umberto Sacripanti, Alberto D'Amario, Giacomo Rossi Stuart, Carlo Pedersoli, Alex Revides, Franco Mancinelli, Patrick Crean, Guidarino Guidi, Diana King, Clelia Metania, Eduard Linkers, Johanna Hofer, Luigi Barzini, Carlo Licari, Angiolo Galassi, Carlo Hintermann, Tiberio Mitri, Eva Kotthaus, Gisella Mathews, Vittorio Jannitti, Peter Illing, Sam Levine.

135

(M-G-M)
DON'T GO NEAR THE WATER

Producer, Lawrence Weingarten; Director, Charles Walters; Screenplay by Dorothy Kingsley and George Wells; Based on Novel by William Brinkley; Music by Bronislau Kaper; Lyrics for Song by Sammy Cahn; Sung by The Lancers; Assistant Director, Al Jennings; Costumes by Helen Rose; An Avon Production in CinemaScope and Metrocolor. December release.

CAST

Lt. Max Siegel	Glenn Ford
Melora	Gia Scala
Adam Garrett	Earl Holliman
Lt. Alice Tomlen	Anne Francis
Gordon Ripwell	Keenan Wynn
Lt. Cmdr. Clinton Nash	Fred Clark
Deborah Aldrich	Eva Gabor
Ensign Tyson	Russ Tamblyn
Lt. Ross Pendleton	Jeff Richards
Farragut Jones	Mickey Shaughnessy
Adm. Boatwright	Howard Smith
Mr. Alba	Romney Brent
Janie	Mary Wickes
Lt. Cmdr. Gladstone	Jack Straw
Lt. Cmdr. Hereford	Robert Nichols
Lt. Cmdr. Diplock	John Alderson
Rep. George Jansen	Jack Albertson
Rep. Arthur Smithfield	Charles Watts

Gia Scala, Romney Brent, Glenn Ford
Top: Jeff Richards, Russ Tamblyn, Glenn Ford,
Fred Clark; Center: Jeff Richards, Eva Gabor,
Russ Tamblyn, Anne Francis

Charles Watts, Glenn Ford, Jack Albertson
Earl Holliman
Top: Earl Holliman, Jeff Richards, Anne Francis
Center: Glenn Ford, Earl Holliman

Marlon Brando
in
"Sayonara"

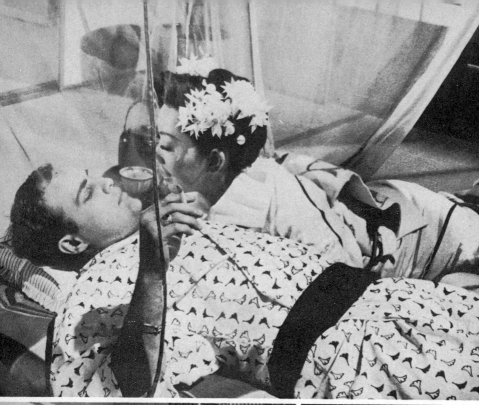

Douglas Watson, Kent Smith, Patricia Owens,
Ricardo Montalban
Top: Marlon Brando, Miiko Taka
Center: Marlon Brando, James Garner,
Kent Smith; Marlon Brando, Miiko Taka

(WARNER BROS.)

SAYONARA

Producer, William Goetz; Director, Joshua
Logan; Screenplay by Paul Osborn; Based on
Novel by James Michener; Assistant Director,
Ad Schaumer; Music by Franz Waxman; Song
by Irving Berlin; Costumes by Norma Koch;
Revue Number Staged by LeRoy Prinz; In
Technirama and Technicolor. December release.

CAST

Major Gruver	Marlon Brando
Nakamura	Ricardo Montalban
Kelly	Red Buttons
Eileen Webster	Patricia Owens
Mrs. Webster	Martha Scott
Bailey	James Garner
Hana-ogi	Miiko Taka
Katsumi	Miyoshi Umeki
General Webster	Kent Smith
Colonel Craford	Douglas Watson
Fumiko-san	Reiko Kuba
Teruko-san	Soo Yong

and Shochiki Kagekidan Girls Revue.

Red Buttons, Miyoshi Umeki
Top: Marlon Brando, James Garner

Marlon Brando, Martha Scott, Kent Smith
Center: Ricardo Montalban, James Garner,
Miiko Taka, Marlon Brando

139

Kim Novak, Frank Sinatra, Rita Hayworth

Top: Frank Sinatra

Kim Novak

140

(COLUMBIA)

PAL JOEY

Producer, Fred Kohlmar; Director, George Sidney; Screenplay by Dorothy Kingsley; From the Musical Play by John O'Hara, Richard Rodgers and Lorenz Hart; Music Adaptation by George Duning and Nelson Riddle; Choreography by Hermes Pan; Gowns by Jean Louis; Assistant Director, Art Black; An Essex-George Sidney Production in Technicolor. December release.

CAST

Vera Simpson	Rita Hayworth
Joey Evans	Frank Sinatra
Linda English	Kim Novak
Gladys	Barbara Nichols
Ned Galvin	Bobby Sherwood
Mike Miggins	Hank Henry
Mrs. Casey	Elizabeth Patterson
Bartender	Robin Morse
Col. Langley	Frank Wilcox
Mr. Forsythe	Pierre Watkin
Anderson	Barry Bernard
Carol	Ellie Kent
Sabrina	Mara McAfee
Patsy	Betty Utey
Lola	Bek Nelson

Top: Frank Sinatra, Rita Hayworth
Right Center: Frank Sinatra, Kim Novak

Kim Novak

(UNITED ARTISTS)

LEGEND OF THE LOST

Producer-Director, Henry Hathaway; Screenplay by Robert Presnell, Jr. and Ben Hecht; Music by A. F. Lavagnino; Assistant Director, Edward Morey, Jr., Joseph Lenzi; Costumes by Gaia Romanini; A Batjac and Dear Film Production in Technirama and Technicolor. December release.

CAST

Joe January	John Wayne
Dita	Sophia Loren
Paul Bonnard	Rossano Brazzi
Prefect Dukas	Kurt Kasznar
Girls	Sonia Moser, Angela Portaluri
Galli Galli	Ibrahim El Hadish

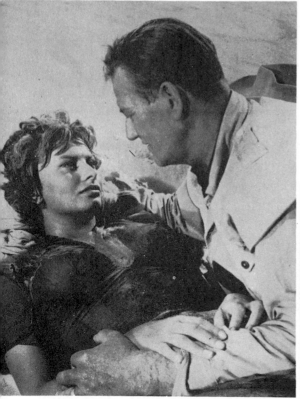

Sophia Loren, John Wayne

Sophia Loren, John Wayne, Rossano Brazzi

Top: John Wayne, Sophia Loren, Rossano Brazzi

142

Alec Guinness
in
"The Bridge On The River Kwai"

(COLUMBIA)

THE BRIDGE ON
THE RIVER KWAI

Producer, Sam Spiegel; Director, David Lean; Screenplay by Pierre Boulle based on his Novel; Assistant Directors, Gus Agosti and Ted Sturgis; Music by Malcolm Arnold; In CinemaScope and Technicolor. December release.

CAST

Shears .... William Holden
Col. Nicholson .... Alec Guinness
Major Warden .... Jack Hawkins
Col. Saito .... Sessue Hayakawa
Maj. Clipton .... James Donald
Lt. Joyce .... Geoffrey Horne
Col. Green .... Andre Morell
Capt. Reeves .... Peter Williams
Major Hughes .... John Boxer
Grogan .... Percy Herbert
Baker .... Harold Goodwin
Nurse .... Ann Sears
Capt. Kanematsu .... Henry Okawa
Lt. Miura .... K. Katsumoto
Yai .... M. R. B. Chakrabandhu
Siamese Girls .... Vilaiwan Seeboonreaung, Ngamta Suphaphongs, Javanart Punynchoti, Kannikar Bowklee.

Top: Geoffrey Horne, Jack Hawkins, William Holden, Sessue Hayakawa
Center: (L) Geoffrey Horne, Sessue Hayakawa (R) Alec Guinness, Sessue Hayakawa, Geoffrey Horne

Jack Hawkins, William Holden, Geoffrey Horne
Center: Alec Guinness, Geoffrey Horne

Geoffrey Horne, Jack Hawkins, William Holden

William Holden, James Donald, Alec Guinness

Top: Alec Guinness, Sessue Hayakawa

(UNIVERSAL)
MY MAN GODFREY

Producer, Ross Hunter; Director, Henry Koster; Screenplay by Everett Freeman, Peter Berneis and William Bowers; Based on Screenplay by Morrie Ryskind and Eric Hatch and on the Novel by Eric Hatch; Gowns by Bill Thomas; Assistant Director, Frank Shaw; Music by Frank Skinner; In CinemaScope and Eastman Color. December release.

CAST

Irene	June Allyson
Godfrey	David Niven
Angelica	Jessie Royce Landis
Mr. Bullock	Robert Keith
Francesca	Eva Gabor
Vincent	Jay Robinson
Cordelia	Martha Hyer
Molly	Jeff Donnell
Hubert	Herbert Anderson
Brent	Eric Sinclair
Lt. O'Connor	Dabbs Greer
Captain	Fred Essler
Elliott	Harry Cheshire
George	Robert Clarke
Howard	William Hudson
Farnsworth	Richard Deacon

and Jack Mather, Paul Levitt, Robert Brubaker, Fred Coby, Voltaire Perkins, Robert Foulk, Thomas B. Henry.

Top, and Right Center: June Allyson, David Niven

Jessie Royce Landis, David Niven

146

(PARAMOUNT)

THE SAD SACK

Producer, Hal B. Wallis; Director, George Marshall; Screenplay by Edmund Beloin and Nate Monaster; Based on Cartoon Character created by George Baker; Costumes by Edith Head; Assistant Director, C. C. Coleman, Jr.; Associate Producer, Paul Nathan; Music by Walter Scharf; Musical Numbers Staged by Charles O'Curran; Song by Hal David and Burt F. Bacharach; In VistaVision. December release.

CAST

Bixby	Jerry Lewis
Dolan	David Wayne
Maj. Shelton	Phyllis Kirk
Abdul	Peter Lorre
Pvt. Stan Wenaslawsky	Joe Mantell
Sgt. Pulley	Gene Evans
Ali Mustapha	George Dolenz
Zita	Liliane Montevecchi
Gen. Vanderlip	Shepperd Strudwick
Hassim	Abraham Sofaer
Sgt. Hansen	Mary Treen
Lt. Wilson	Drew Cahill
Moki	Michael Ansara
Capt. Ward	Don Haggerty
French General	Jean Del Val
Arab Chieftain	Dan Seymour
Hazel	Yvette Vickers

Top: Jerry Lewis, Marilyn Hanold
Right center: Jerry Lewis, David Wayne, Joe Mantell

Jerry Lewis, Phyllis Kirk

Anthony Franciosa, Anna Magnani, Joseph Calleia

(PARAMOUNT)

WILD IS THE WIND

Producer, Hal B. Wallis; Director, George Cukor; Screenplay and Story by Arnold Schulman; Based on Story by Vittorio Nino Novarese; Costumes by Edith Head; Assistant Director, D. Michael Moore; Associate Producer, Paul Nathan; Music by Dimitri Tiomkin; Songs by Dimitri Tiomkin and Ned Washington sung by Johnny Mathis, and by Fernando Albano and Pacifico Vento sung by Anna Magnani; In VistaVision. December release.

CAST

Gioia	Anna Magnani
Gino	Anthony Quinn
Bene	Anthony Franciosa
Angie	Dolores Hart
Alberto	Joseph Calleia
Teresa	Lili Valenty
Wool Buyer	James Flavin
Priest	Dick Ryan
Party Guests	Iphigenie Castiglioni, Joseph Vitale, Ruth Lee, Frances Morris

Anthony Franciosa, Anna Magnani, Anthony Quinn
Center: Dolores Hart, Anthony Quinn

Top: Anna Magnani, Anthony Quinn
Center: (L): Anna Magnani, Anthony Franciosa

149

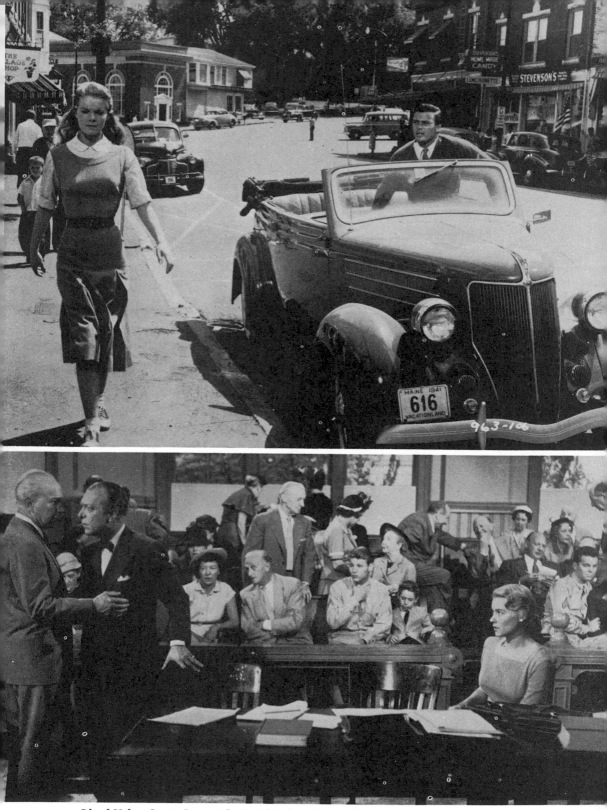

Lloyd Nolan, Staats Cotsworth, David Nelson, Scotty Morrow, Hope Lange, Russ Tamblyn,
Diane Varsi; Top: Diane Varsi, Barry Coe

Lana Turner

(20th CENTURY-FOX)

PEYTON PLACE

Producer, Jerry Wald; Director, Mark Robson; Screenplay by John Michael Hayes; Based on Novel by Grace Metalious; Music by Franz Waxman; Assistant Director, Hal Herman; Wardrobe by Charles LeMaire; Costumes by Adele Palmer; In CinemaScope and DeLuxe Color. December release.

CAST

Constance	Lana Turner
Selena Cross	Hope Lange
Michael Rossi	Lee Philips
Dr. Swain	Lloyd Nolan
Lucas Cross	Arthur Kennedy
Norman Page	Russ Tamblyn
Allison	Diane Varsi
Betty Anderson	Terry Moore
Rodney Harrington	Barry Coe
Nellie Cross	Betty Field
Ted Carter	David Nelson
Mrs. Thornton	Mildred Dunnock
Harrington	Leon Ames
Prosecutor	Lorne Greene
Seth Bushwell	Robert H. Harris
Margie	Tami Conner
Charles Partridge	Staats Cotsworth
Marion Partridge	Peg Hillias
Mrs. Page	Erin O'Brien-Moore
Joey Cross	Scotty Morrow
Paul Cross	Bill Lundmark
Matt	Alan Reed, Jr.
Pee Wee	Kip King
Kathy	Steffi Sidney

Top: (L) Hope Lange, Betty Field, Arthur Kennedy; (R) Barry Coe, Terry Moore, Leon Ames
Center: (L) Russ Tamblyn, Diane Varsi; (R) Lana Turner, Lloyd Nolan, Lee Philips

151

Lana Turner, Lee Philips   Russ Tamblyn, Diane Varsi

David Nelson, Hope Lange, Diane Varsi
Center: Hope Lange, Russ Tamblyn, Diane
Varsi, David Nelson, Lloyd Nolan

Lana Turner, Hope Lange
Center: Hope Lange, Diane Varsi

Diane Varsi   Terry Moore, Barry Coe   Betty Field

Lana Turner, Betty Field   Lee Philips, Lana Turner, Diane Varsi
Center: Hope Lange, Arthur Kennedy   Center: Diane Varsi, Barry Coe

(20th CENTURY-FOX)

KISS THEM FOR ME

Producer, Jerry Wald; Director, Stanley Donen; Screenplay by Julius Epstein; Based on Play by Luther Davis and Novel by Frederic Wakeman; Music by Lionel Newman; Song by Lionel Newman and Caroll Coates; Sung by The McGuire Sisters; Assistant Director, David Hall; Wardrobe, Charles Le-Maire; In CinemaScope and DeLuxe Color. December release.

CAST

Crewson	Cary Grant
Alice	Jayne Mansfield
Eddie Turnbill	Leif Erickson
Gwenneth	Suzy Parker
Lt. "Mac" McCann	Ray Walston
Mississip	Larry Blyden
CPO Ruddle	Nathaniel Frey
Commander Wallace	Werner Klemperer
Ensign Lewis	Jack Mullaney
RAF Pilot	Ben Wright
Gunner	Michael Ross
Roundtree	Harry Carey, Jr.
Neilson	Frank Nelson
Debbie	Caprice Yordan
Lucille	Ann McCrea

Left: Cary Grant, Suzy Parker, Ray Walston

Top: Ann McCrea, Larry Blyden, Jayne Mansfield, Werner Klemperer, Ray Montgomery, Cary Grant, Nathaniel Frey, Ray Walston

(M-G-M)

SADDLE THE WIND

Producer, Armand Deutsch; Director, Robert Parrish; Screenplay by Rod Serling; Based on Story by Thomas Thompson; In CinemaScope. December release.

CAST

Steve Sinclair	Robert Taylor
Joan Blake	Julie London
Tony Sinclair	John Cassavetes
Mr. Deneen	Donald Crisp
Larry Venables	Charles McGraw
Clay Ellison	Royal Dano
Mrs. Ellison	Irene Tedrow
Dallas Hansen	Richard Erdman
Hamp	Ray Teal
Brick	Douglas Spencer

Douglas Spencer, Royal Dano, Donald Crisp
Center: John Cassavetes, Julie London, Robert Taylor

Center: John Cassavetes, Robert Taylor

(DCA)

THE GOLDEN AGE OF COMEDY

Produced and Written by Robert Youngson; Narrated by Dwight Weist and Ward Wilson; Music by George Steiner; Released by Distributors Corporation of America in December. A cavalcade of screen humor from films made during the middle and late 'twenties with Laurel and Hardy, Will Rogers, Carole Lombard, Jean Harlow, Ben Turpin, Harry Langdon, Charlie Chase, Billy Bevan, Edgar Kennedy, Andy Clyde, Charlie Murray, Harry Gribbon, Cameo, The Keystone Cops.

Top: Carole Lombard
Center: Stan Laurel, Jean Harlow, Oliver Hardy

Madeline Hurlock
Top: Ben Turpin
Center: Will Rogers, Mack Sennett

 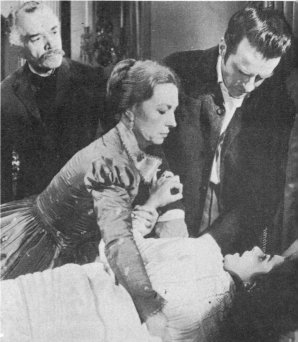

 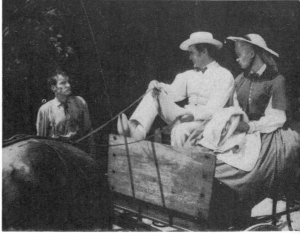

Montgomery Clift, Elizabeth Taylor
Top: (L) Elizabeth Taylor, Eva Marie Saint
(R) Lee Marvin, Montgomery Clift, Nigel Patrick

Montgomery Clift, Rod Taylor, Eva Marie Saint
Center: Walter Abel, Agnes Moorehead,
Montgomery Clift, Elizabeth Taylor

(M-G-M)

RAINTREE COUNTY

Producer, David Lewis; Director, Edward Dmytryk; Screenplay by Millard Kaufman, Associate Producer; Based on Novel by Ross Lockridge, Jr.; Music by Johnny Green; Song Sung by Nat "King" Cole; Costumes by Walter Plunkett; Assistant Director, Ridgeway Callow; In Technicolor. December release.

CAST

John Wickliff Shawnessy	Montgomery Clift
Susanna Drake	Elizabeth Taylor
Nell Gaither	Eva Marie Saint
Jerusalem Webster Stiles	Nigel Patrick
Orville "Flash" Perkins	Lee Marvin
Garwood B. Jones	Rod Taylor
Ellen Shawnessy	Agnes Moorehead
T. D. Shawnessy	Walter Abel
Barbara Drake	Jarma Lewis
Bobby Drake	Tom Drake
Ezra Gray	Rhys Williams
Niles Foster	Russell Collins
Southern Officer	DeForest Kelley

Top: Agnes Moorehead, Nigel Patrick,
Eva Marie Saint, Rod Taylor
Left: Elizabeth Taylor
Right: Montgomery Clift

Myrna Hansen, Nigel Patrick, Montgomery Clift,
Elizabeth Taylor

Jarma Lewis, Montgomery Clift,
Elizabeth Taylor, Tom Drake

Anthony Quinn

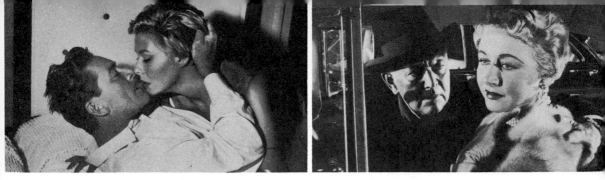

Errol Flynn, Rossana Rory
in "The Big Boodle"

Sidney Blackmer, Vera Ralston
in "Accused of Murder"

THE BIG BOODLE (UNITED ARTISTS) Producer, Lewis Blumberg; Director, Richard Wilson; Screenplay by Jo Eisenger; Based on Novel by Robert Sylvester; Music by Paul Lavista; Assistant Director, Henry Hartman; January release. CAST: Errol Flynn, Pedro Armendariz, Rossana Rory, Gia Scala, Sandro Giglio, Jacques Aubuchon, Carlos Rivas, Charles Todd, Guillerme Alvarez Guedes, Carlos Mas, Rogelio Hernandez, Velia Martinez, Aurora Pita.

FIVE STEPS TO DANGER (UNITED ARTISTS) Producer-Director, Henry S. Kesler; Screenplay by Henry S. Kesler; Story by Donald Hamilton and Turnley Walker; Based on Serial by Donald Hamilton; Music by Paul Sawtell and Bert Shefter; Assistant Director, Horace Hough; Wardrobe, Adele Parmenter and Einar Bourman; January release. CAST: Ruth Roman, Sterling Hayden, Werner Klemperer, Richard Gaines, Charles Davis, Jeanne Cooper, Peter Hansen, Karl Lindt, John Mitchum, John Merrick.

RIDE THE HIGH IRON (COLUMBIA) Producer, William Self; Director, Don Weis; Screenplay by Milton Gelman; Assistant Director, Paul Helmick; Wardrobe, Gerry Bos; Music by Melvin Lenard; January release. CAST: Don Taylor, Sally Forrest, Raymond Burr, Lisa Golm, Otto Waldis, Nestor Paiva, Mae Clark, Maureen Marsac, Robert Johnson.

ACCUSED OF MURDER (REPUBLIC) Producer-Director, Joe Kane; Screenplay by Bob Williams and W. R. Burnett; From Novel "Vanity Row" by W. R. Burnett; Music by R. Dale Butts; Song by Herb Newman and Buddy Bregman; Assistant Director, Virgil Hart; January release. CAST: David Brian, Vera Ralston, Sidney Blackmer, Virginia Grey, Warren Stevens, Lee Van Cleef, Barry Kelley, Richard Karlan, Frank Puglia, Elisha Cook, Ian MacDonald, Greta Thyssen, Claire Carleton, Hank Worden.

NAKED PARADISE (AMERICAN-INTERNATIONAL) Producer-Director, Roger Corman; Executive Producer, James H. Nicholson; Screenplay by Charles B. Griffith and Mark Hanna; Assistant Director, Lou Place; Wardrobe, Shaheen of Honolulu; Music by Ronald Stein; Other songs by Alvin Kaleolani; January release. CAST: Richard Denning, Beverly Garland, Lisa Montell, Leslie Bradley, Richard Miller, Jonathan Haze.

DUEL AT APACHE WELLS (REPUBLIC) Producer-Director, Joe Kane; Screenplay by Bob Williams; Assistant Director, Herb Mendelson; Costumes, Alexis Davidoff; A Naturama Picture. January release. CAST: Anna Maria Alberghetti, Ben Cooper, Jim Davis, Harry Shannon, Francis J. McDonald, Bob Steele, Frank Puglia, Argentina Brunetti, Ian MacDonald, John Dierkes, Ric Roman.

Sally Forrest, Raymond Burr, Don Taylor
in "Ride The High Iron"

Frank Puglia, Eva Novak, Rosa Turich, Anna Maria Alberghetti, Ben Cooper, Tudor Owen, Argentina Brunetti, Rocky Shahan in "Duel At Apache Wells"

FOUR BOYS AND A GUN (UNITED ARTISTS) Producer-Director, William Berke; Screenplay by Philip Yordan and Leo Townsend; Based on Novel by Willard Wiener; Music by Albert Glasser; Song by Stanley Rubin and His Tigertown Five; Assistant Directors, George Ackerson and John Bowman; A Security Pictures Production; January release. CAST: Frank Sutton, Tarry Green, James Franciscus, William Hinant, Otto Hulett, Robert Dryden, J. Pat O'Malley, Diana Herbert, Patricia Sloan, Nancy Devlin, Patricia Bosworth, David Burns, Anne Seymour, Frank Gero, Noel Glass, Karl Swenson, Lisa Osten, Sid Raymond, George McIver, Frank Campanella.

FLESH AND THE SPUR (AMERICAN-INTERNATIONAL) Producer, Alex Gordon, Executive Producers, Charles J. Lyons, Jr. and Touch Connors; Director, Edward L. Cahn; Story and Screenplay by Charles B. Griffith and Mark Hanna; Song by Ross Bagdasarian; Music by Ronald Stein; Wardrobe by Stan Kufel; A Hy Production; January release. CAST: John Agar, Marla English, Touch Connors, Raymond Hatton, Maria Monay, Joyce Meadows, Kenne Duncan, Frank Lackteen, Mel Gaines, Michael Harris, Eddie Kafafian, Richard Alexander, Kermit Maynard, Bud Osborn, Buddy Roosevelt.

Alan Dale
in "Don't Knock The Rock"

Merry Anders, Harry Jackson, Ray Danton
in "The Night Runner"

DON'T KNOCK THE ROCK (COLUMBIA) Producer, Sam Katzman; Director, Fred F. Sears; Screenplay by Robert E. Kent and James B. Gordon; Assistant Director, Sam Nelson; Dances Staged and Created by Earl Barton; A Clover Production; January release. CAST: Bill Haley and His Comets, Alan Dale, Alan Freed, The Treniers, Little Richard, Dave Appell and His Applejacks, Patricia Hardy, Fay Baker, Jana Lund, Gail Ganley, Pierre Watkin, George Cisar, Dick Elliott, Jovada and Jimmy Ballard.

CHAIN OF EVIDENCE (ALLIED ARTISTS) Producer, Ben Schwalb; Director, Paul Landres; Screenplay by Elwood Ullman; Assistant Director, Don Torpin; Music by Marlin Skiles; Wardrobe by Bert Henrikson; January release. CAST: Bill Elliott, James Lydon, Don Haggerty, Claudia Barrett, Tina Carver, Ross Elliott, Meg Randall, Timothy Carey, John Bleifer, Dabbs Greer, John Close, Hugh Sanders.

HOT SHOTS (ALLIED ARTISTS) Producer, Ben Schwalb; Director, Jean Yarbrough; Screenplay by Jack Townley and Elwood Ullman; Story by Jack Townley; Assistant Director, Don Torpin; Music by Marlin Skiles; Wardrobe by Bert Henrikson; February release. CAST: Huntz Hall, Stanley Clements, Phil Phillips, Joi Lansing, Robert Shayne, Henry Rowland, Mark Dana, Queenie Smith, David Condon, Jimmy Murphy, Isabel Randolph.

ATTACK OF THE CRAB MONSTER (ALLIED ARTISTS) Producer-Director, Roger Corman; Associate Producer, Charles Griffith; Screenplay by Charles Griffith; Assistant Director, Maurice Vaccarino; Music by Ronald Stein; February release. CAST: Richard Garland, Pamela Duncan, Russell Johnson, Leslie Bradley, Mel Welles, Richard Cutting, Beech Dickerson, Tony Miller, Ed Nelson.

NOT OF THIS EARTH (ALLIED ARTISTS) Producer-Director, Roger Gorman; Screenplay by Charles Griffith and Mark Hanna; Music by Ronald Stein; Assistant Director, Lou Place; February release. CAST: Paul Birch, Beverly Garland, Morgan Jones, William Roerick, Jonathan Haze, Richard Miller, Anne Carroll, Pat Flynn, Roy Engel, Tamar Cooper, Harold Fong, Gail Ganley, Ralph Reed.

HIGH TERRACE (ALLIED ARTISTS) Producer, Robert S. Baker; Director, Henry Cass; Screenplay by Alfred Shaughnessy and Norman Hudis; Adapted by Brock Williams from a Story by A. T. Weisman; Music by Stanley Black; A Cipa Production; February release. CAST: Dale Robertson, Lois Maxwell, Derek Bond, Eric Pohlmann, Mary Laura Wood, Lionel Jeffries, Jameson Clark, Carl Bernard, Garard Green, Olwen Brookes, Benita Lydal, Marianne Stone, Frederick Treves, Jonathan Field, Gretchen Franklin, Alan Robinson, Jack Cunningham.

John Gavin, Grant Williams, Gia Scala, Elsa
Martinelli in "Four Girls In Town"

Cornell Borchers, Errol Flynn
in "Istanbul"

FOUR GIRLS IN TOWN (UNIVERSAL) Producer, Aaron Rosenberg; Directed and Written by Jack Sher; Gowns, Rosemary Odell; Assistant Directors, Dick Mayberry and Wilbur Mosier; "Rhapsody" composed by Alex North; In CinemaScope and Technicolor; January release. CAST: George Nader, Julie Adams, Marianne Cook, Elsa Martinelli, Gia Scala, Sydney Chaplin, Grant Williams, John Gavin, Herbert Anderson, Hy Auerbach, Ainslie Pryor, Judson Pratt, James Bell, Mabel Albertson, Dave Barry, Maurice Marsac, Helene Stanton, Irene Corlett, Eugene Mazzola.

ISTANBUL (UNIVERSAL) Producer, Albert J. Cohen; Director, Joseph Pevney; Screenplay by Seton I. Miller, Barbara Gray and Richard Alan Simmons; Story by Seton I. Miller; Music by Jay Livingston, Ray Evans and Victor Young; Gowns by Bill Thomas; Assistant Director, Joseph E. Kenny; In CinemaScope and Technicolor; February release. CAST: Errol Flynn, Cornell Borchers, John Bentley, Torin Thatcher, Leif Erickson, Peggy Knudsen, Martin Benson, Nat "King" Cole, Werner Klemperer, Vladimir Sokoloff, Jan Arvan, Nico Minardos, Ted Hecht, David Bond, Roland Varno, Hillevi Rombin.

Chuck Connors, John Smith
in "Tomahawk Trail"

Doris Singleton, John Lund, Angela Greene
in "Affair In Reno"

TOMAHAWK TRAIL (UNITED ARTISTS) Executive Producer. Aubrey Schenck; Producer Howard W. Koch; Director, Lesley Selander; Music, Les Baxter; Screenplay by David Chandler; Assistant Director, Paul Wurtzel; Wardrobe, Wesley V. Jefferies and Angela Alexander; A Bel-Air Production; February release. CAST: Chuck Connors, John Smith, Susan Cummings, Lisa Montell, George Neise, Robert Knapp, Eddie Little, Frederick Ford, Dean Stanton.

UTAH BLAINE (COLUMBIA) Producer, Sam Katzman; Director, Fred F. Sears; Screenplay by Robert E. Kent and James B. Gordon; Based on Novel by Louis L'Amour; Assistant Director, Willard Sheldon; A Clover Production; February release. CAST: Rory Calhoun, Susan Cummings, Angela Stevens, Max Baer, Paul Langton, George Keymas, Ray Teal, Gene Roth, Norman Fredric, Ken Christy, Steve Darrell, Terry Frost, Dennis Moore, Jack Ingram.

HOT SUMMER NIGHT (M-G-M) Producer, Morton Fine; Director, David Friedkin; Screenplay by Morton Fine and David Friedkin; Based on Story by Edwin P. Hicks; Music by Andre Previn; Assistant Director, Joel Freeman; February release. CAST: Leslie Nielsen, Colleen Miller, Edward Andrews, Jay C. Flippen, James Best, Paul Richards, Robert Wilke, Claude Akins, Marianne Stewart.

AFFAIR IN RENO (REPUBLIC) Producer, Sidney Picker; Director, R. G. Springsteen; Screenplay by John K. Butler; Story by Gerald Drayson Adams; Music, R. Dale Butts; Assistant Director, Leonard Kunody; Costumes, Alexis Davidoff; A Naturama Picture; February release. CAST: John Lund, Doris Singleton, John Archer, Angela Greene, Alan Hale, Harry Bartell, Howard McNear, Richard Deacon, Thurston Hall, Billy Vincent, Eddie Foster.

THE NIGHT RUNNNER (UNIVERSAL) Producer, Albert J. Cohen; Director, Abner Biberman; Screenplay by Gene Levitt; Based on Story by Owen Cameron; Gowns by Rosemary Odell; Assistant Directors, George Lollier and James Welch; February release. CAST: Ray Danton, Colleen Miller, Merry Anders, Willis Bouchey, Harry Jackson, Robert Anderson, Jean Inness, Eddy C. Waller, John Stephenson, Alexander Campbell, Natalie Masters, Richard Cutting, Steve Pendleton, Jack Lomas.

VOODOO ISLAND (UNITED ARTISTS) Executive Producer, Aubrey Schenck; Producer, Howard W. Koch; Director, Reginald Le Borg; Screenplay by Richard Landau; Music, Les Baxter; Assistant Director, Paul Wurtzel; A Bel-Air Production. February release. CAST: Boris Karloff, Beverly Tyler, Murvyn Vye, Elisha Cook, Rhodes Reason, Jean Engstrom, Frederich Ledebur, Glenn Dixon, Owen Cunningham, Herbert Patterson, Jerome Frank.

James Best, Leslie Nielsen, Coleen Miller
in "Hot Summer Night"

Lois Maxwell, Dale Robertson
in "High Terrace"

PHARAOH'S CURSE (UNITED ARTISTS) Executive Producer, Aubrey Schenck; Producer, Howard W. Koch; Director, Lee Sholem; Story and Screenplay by Richard Landau; Music by Les Baxter; Assistant Director, Paul Wurtzel; Wardrobe by Wesley V. Jefferies and Angela Alexander; A Bel-Air Production; February release. CAST: Mark Dana, Ziva Shapir, Diane Brewster, George Neise, Alvaro Guillot, Ben Wright, Guy Prescott, Terence deMarney, Richard Peel, Kurt Katch, Robert Fortin, Ralph Clanton.

THE STORM RIDER (20th CENTURY-FOX) Producer, Bernard Glasser; Director, Edward Bernds; Screenplay by Edward Bernds and Don Martin from Novel by L. L. Foreman; Music by Les Baxter; a Regalscope Film; March release. CAST: Scott Brady, Mala Powers, Bill Williams, Olin Howlin, William Fawcett, John Goddard, Hank Patterson, James Dobson, John Close, Jim Hayward, Cortland Shepard, Rocky Shahan, Frank Richards. Rick Vallin, Ronald Foster, Tom London, Britt Wood, Al Baffert, Rocky Lundy, John Cason, Bud Osborne, Roy Engel, George Keymas, Lane Chandler, Jean Ann Lewis, Wayne Mallory.

"The Delinquents"

Vince Edwards, Cleo Moore
in "Hit And Run"

THE DELINQUENTS (UNITED ARTISTS) Produced, Directed and Written by Robert Altman; Assistant Director, Reza Badiyi; An Imperial Production: March release. CAST: Tom Laughlin, Peter Miller, Richard Bakalyn, Rosemary Howard, Helene Hawley, Leonard Belove, Lotus Corelli, James Lantz, Christine Altman, George Kuhn, Pat Stedman, Norman Zands, James Leria, Jet Pinkston, Kermit Echols, Joe Adleman.

HELL'S CROSSROADS (REPUBLIC) Producer, Rudy Ralston; Director, Franklin Adreon; Screenplay by John K. Butler and Barry Shipman; Story by John K. Butler; Assistant Director, Roy Wade; A Naturama Picture; March release. CAST: Stephen McNally, Peggie Castle, Robert Vaughn, Barton MacLane, Harry Shannon, Henry Brandon, Douglas Kennedy, Grant Withers, Myron Healey, Frank Wilcox, Jean Howell, Morris Ankrum.

ZOMBIES OF MORA-TAU (COLUMBIA) Producer, Sam Katzman; Director, Edward Cahn; Screenplay by Raymond T. Marcus; Story by George Plympton; Assistant Director, Jerrold Bernstein; A Clover Production; March release. CAST: Gregg Palmer, Allison Hayes, Autumn Russell, Joel Ashley, Morris Ankrum, Marjorie Eaton, Gene Roth, Leonard Geer, Karl Davis, William Baskin, Lewis Webb, Ray Corrigan, Mel Curtis, Frank Hagny.

THE MAN WHO TURNED TO STONE (COLUMBIA) Producer, Sam Katzman; Director, Leslie Kardos; Screenplay by Raymond T. Marcus; Assistant Director, Sam Nelson; A Clover Production; March release. CAST: Victor Jory, Ann Doran, Charlotte Austin, William Hudson, Paul Cavanagh, Tina Carver, Jean Willes, Victor Varconi, Frederick Ledubur, George Lynn, Barbara Wilson.

HOLD THAT HYPNOTIST (ALLIED ARTISTS) Producer, Ben Schwalb; Director, Austen Jewell; Screenplay by Dan Pepper; Assistant Director, Edward Morey, Jr.; Music by Marlin Skiles; Wardrobe by Bert Henrikson; March release. CAST: Huntz Hall, Stanley Clements. Jane Nigh, Robert Foulk, James Flavin, Mel Welles, Queenie Smith, David Condon, Jimmy Murphy, Murray Alper, Dick Elliott.

HIT AND RUN (UNITED ARTISTS) Produced, Directed and Written by Hugo Haas; Associate Producer, Robert Erlik; Music by Franz Steininger; Based on Story by Herbert Q. Phillips; Assistant Director, Leon Chooluck; Gowns by Emerson; Song sung by Ella Mae Morse; March release. CAST: Hugo Haas, Cleo Moore, Vince Edwards, Dolores Reed, Mari Lea, Pat Goldin, Carl Militaire, Robert Cassidy, Julie Mitchum, John Zaremba, Steve Mitchel, Jan Englund, Dick Paxton.

Frances Helm, Gregg Palmer
in "Revolt At Fort Laramie"

Touch Connors, Mary Ellen Kay
in "Voodoo Woman"

REVOLT AT FORT LARAMIE (UNITED ARTISTS) Executive Producer, Aubrey Schenck; Producer, Howard W. Koch; Director, Lesley Selander; Screenplay by Robert C. Dennis; Music by Les Baxter; Assistant Director, Paul Wurtzel; Wardrobe, Wesley V. Jefferies and Angela Alexander; A Bel-Air Production in DeLuxe Color; March release. CAST: John Dehner, Gregg Palmer, Frances Helm, Don Gordon, Robert Keys, William "Bill" Phillips, Cain Mason, Robert Knapp, Eddie Little, Dean Stanton, Bill Barker, Clay Randolph, Kenne Duncan, Frederick Ford.

VOODOO WOMAN (AMERICAN-INTERNATIONAL) Executive Producers, Samuel Z. Arkoff and James H. Nicholson; Producer, Alex Gordon; Director, Edward L. Cahn; Story and Screenplay by Russell Bender and V. I. Voss; Music by Darrell Calker; Song by John Blackburn and Darrell Calker; A Carmel Production; March release. CAST: Marla English, Tom Conway, Touch Connors, Lance Fuller, Mary Ellen Kaye, Paul Dubov, Martin Wilkins, Norman Willis, Otis Greene, Emmett E. Smith, Paul Blaisdell, Giselle D'Arc, Jean Davis.

**Albert Dekker, Jack Kelly, Mari Blanchard
in "She Devil"**

**Forrest Tucker, Eva Bartok
in "Break In The Circle"**

THE UNDEAD (AMERICAN-INTERNATIONAL) Producer-Director, Robert Corman; Assistant Director, Lou Place; Music by Ronald Stein; Screenplay by Charles Griffith and Mark Hanna; March release. CAST: Pamela Duncan, Richard Garland, Allison Hayes, Val DuFour, Mel Welles, Dorothy Neuman, Billy Barty, Bruno Ve Soto, Aaron Saxon, Richard Devon.

THE QUIET GUN (20th CENTURY-FOX) Producer, Earle Lyon; Director, William Claxton; Screenplay by Eric Norden; Music by Paul Dunlap; A Regal Film; March release. CAST: Forrest Tucker, Mara Corday, Jim Davis. Kathleen Crowley, Lee Van Cleef, Tom Brown, Lewis Martin, Hank Worden, Gerald Milton, Everett Glass, Edith Evanson.

THE RIVER'S EDGE (20th CENTURY-FOX) Producer, Benedict Bogeaus; Director, Allan Dwan; Screenplay by Harold Jacob Smith and James Leicester, from Smith's Novel "The Highest Mountain"; Music by Louis Forbes; Songs by Louis Forbes and Bobby Troup; Sung by Bob Winn; In DeLuxe Color; March release. CAST: Ray Milland. Anthony Quinn, Debra Paget, Harry Carey, Jr., Chubby Johnson, Bryon Foulger, Tom McKee, Frank Gerstle.

THE BREAK IN THE CIRCLE (20th CENTURY-FOX) Producer, Michael Carreras; Director, Val Guest; Screenplay by Val Guest, based on Novel by Philip Loraine; Music by Doreen Carwithen; April release. CAST: Forrest Tucker, Eva Bartok, Marius Goring, Guy Middleton, Eric Pohlmann, Arnold Marle, Fred Johnson, David King-Wood, Reginald Beckwith.

SHE DEVIL (20th CENTURY-FOX) Producer-Director. Kurt Neumann; Screenplay by Carroll Young and Kurt Neumann, from "The Adaptive Ultimate" by John Jessel; Music by Paul Sawtell and Bert Shefter; A Regal Production; April release. CAST: Albert Dekker, Jack Kelly, Mari Blanchard, Blossom Rock, John Archer, Fay Baker, Paul Cavanagh, George Baxter, Helen Jay, Joan Bradshaw, Tod Griffin.

KRONOS (20th CENTURY-FOX) Producers, Kurt Neumann, Jack Rabin, Irving Block and Louis DeWitt; Director, Kurt Neumann; Screenplay by Lawrence Louis Goldman; Story by Irving Block; Music by Paul Sawtell and Bert Shefter; A Regalscope Film; April release. CAST: Jeff Morrow, Barbara Lawrence, John Emery, George O'Hanlon, Morris Ankrum, Kenneth Alton, John Parrish, Jose Gonzales, Richard Harrison, Marjorie Stapp, Robert Shayne, Donald Eitner, Gordon Mills, John Halloran.

**Joan Taylor, Lex Barker
in "War Drums"**

**Katy Jurado, Mona Freeman, Casey Adams,
Barry Sullivan in "Dragoon Wells Massacre"**

WAR DRUMS (UNITED ARTISTS) Executive Producer, Aubrey Schenck; Producer, Howard W. Koch; Screenplay by Gerald Drayson Adams; Music by Les Baxter; Director, Reginald LeBorg; Assistant Director, Paul Wurtzel; Costumes, Paula Giokaris; A Bel-Air Production in DeLuxe Color; April release. CAST: Lex Barker, Joan Taylor, Ben Johnson, Larry Chance Richard Cutting, James Parnell, John Pickard, John Colicos, Tom Monroe, Jil Jarmyn, Jeanne Carmen, Mauritz Hugo, Ward Ellis, Fred Sherman, Paul Fierro, Alex Montoya, Stuart Whitman, Barbara Parry, Jack Hupp, Red Morgan, Monie Freeman.

DRAGOON WELLS MASSACRE (ALLIED ARTISTS) Producer, Lindsley Parsons; Associate Producer, John H. Burrows; Director, Harold Schuster; Screenplay by Warren Douglas; Story by Oliver Drake; Assistant Directors, Kenneth Walters and Lindsley Parsons, Jr.; Music by Paul Dunlap; Wardrobe by Russell Hanlin; In CinemaScope and DeLuxe Color; April release. CAST: Barry Sullivan, Dennis O'Keefe, Mona Freeman, Katy Jurado, Sebastian Cabot. Casey Adams, Jack Elam, Trevor Bardette, Jon Shepodd. Hank Worden, Warren Douglas, Judy Stranges, Alma Beltran, John War Eagle.

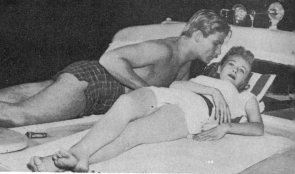

**Carolyn Craig, Nick Adams, John Derek
in "Fury At Showdown"**

**Grant Williams, Randy Stuart
in "The Incredible Shrinking Man"**

FURY AT SHOWDOWN (UNITED ARTISTS) Executive Producer, Robert Goldstein; Producer, John Beck; Director, Gerd Oswald; Screenplay by Jason James; Based on Novel by Lucas Todd; Music by Henry Sukman; Wardrobe. Albert Deano; April release. CAST: John Derek, John Smith, Carolyn Craig, Nick Adams, Gage Clarke, Robert E. Griffin, Malcolm Atterbury, Rusty Lane, Sydney Smith, Frances Morris, Tyler McDuff, Robert Adler, Norman Leavitt, Ken Christy, Tom McKee.

THE IRON SHERIFF (UNITED ARTISTS) Producer, Jerome C. Robinson; Director, Sidney Salkow; Screenplay by Seeleg Lester; Music by Emil Newman; Assistant Director, Ralph E. Black; Wardrobe, Einar Bourman; A Grand Production; April release. CAST: Sterling Hayden, Constance Ford, John Dehner, Kent Taylor, Darryl Hickman, Walter Sande, Frank Ferguson, King Donovan, Mort Mills, Peter Miller, Kathy Nolan, I. Stanford Jolley, Will Wright, Ray Walker, Bob Williams.

THE PHANTOM STAGECOACH (COLUMBIA) Producer, Wallace MacDonald; Director, Ray Nazarro; Screenplay by David Lang; Assistant Director, Jerrold Bernstein; April release. CAST: William Bishop, Kathleen Crowley, Richard Webb, Hugh Sanders, John Doucette, Frank Ferguson, Ray Teal, Percy Helton, Maudie Prickett, Lane Bradford, John Lehmann, Eddy Waller, Robert Anderson.

FOOTSTEPS IN THE NIGHT (ALLIED ARTISTS) Producer, Ben Schwalb: Director, Jean Yarbrough; Screenplay by Albert Band and Elwood Ullman; Story by Albert Band; Assistant Director, Edward Morey, Jr.; Music by Marlin Skiles; Wardrobe by Bert Henrikson; April release. CAST: Bill Elliott, Don Haggerty, Eleanore Tanin, Douglas Dick, Robert Shayne, James Flavin, Gregg Palmer, Harry Tyler, Ann Griffith.

THE INCREDIBLE SHRINKING MAN (UNIVERSAL) Producer, Albert Zugsmith; Director, Jack Arnold; Screenplay by Richard Matheson from his Novel; Gowns by Jay A. Morley Jr.; Assistant Director. William Holland; April release. CAST: Grant Williams, Randy Stuart, April Kent, Paul Langton, Raymond Bailev. William Schall, Frank Scannell, Helene Marshal, Diana Darrin, Billy Curtis.

ROCK ALL NIGHT (AMERICAN-INTERNATIONAL) Executive Producer, James H. Nicholson; Producer-Director, Roger Corman; Screenplay by Charles B. Griffith; Based on Story by David P. Harmon; A Sunset Production; April release. CAST: Dick Miller, Abby Dalton, The Platters, The Blockbusters, Robin Morse, Richard Cutting, Bruno VeSota, Chris Alcaide, Mel Welles, Barboura Morris, Clegg Hoyt, Russell Johnson, Jonathan Haze, Richard Carlan, Jack DeWitt, Bert Nelson, Beech Dickerson, Ed Nelson.

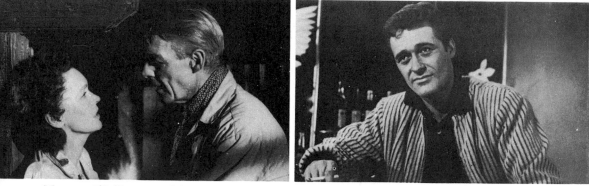

**Maureen O'Sullivan, Randolph Scott
in "The Tall T"**

**Dick Miller
in "Rock All Night"**

THE TALL T (COLUMBIA) Producer, Harry Joe Brown; Associate Producer, Randolph Scott; Director, Budd Boetticher; Assistant to Producer, David Breen; Screenplay by Burt Kennedy; Based on Story by Elmore Leonard; Music by Heinz Roemheld; Assistant Director, Sam Nelson; A Scott-Brown Production in Technicolor; April release. CAST: Randolph Scott, Richard Boone, Maureen O'Sullivan, Arthur Hunnicutt, Skip Homeier, Henry Silva, John Hubbard, Robert Burton, Robert Anderson, Fred E. Sherman, Chris Olsen.

DRAGSTRIP GIRL (AMERICAN-INTERNATIONAL) Executive Producer, Samuel Z. Arkoff; Producer, Alex Gordon; Director, Edward L. Cahn; Story and Screenplay by Lou Rusoff; Music by Ronald Stein; A Golden State Production; April release. CAST: Fay Spain, Steve Terrell, John Ashley, Frank Gorshin. Russ Bender, Tommy Ivo, Gracia Narciso, Tito Vuolo, Dorothy Bruce, Don Shelton, Carla Merey. Leon Tyler, George Dockstader, Bill Welsh, Edmund Cobb, Woody Lee, Judy Bamber.

George Montgomery, Bobby Clark,
Ann Robinson in "Gun Duel In Durango"

Anthony Quinn, Ellen Hope Monroe
in "The Ride Back"

SPOILERS OF THE FOREST (REPUBLIC) Producer-Director, Joe Kane; Screenplay by Bruce Manning; Assistant Director, Leonard Kunody; Costumes, Alexis Davidoff; A Naturama Picture in Trucolor; April release. CAST: Rod Cameron, Vera Ralston, Ray Collins, Hillary Brooke, Edgar Buchanan, Carl Benton Reid, Sheila Bromley, Hank Worden, John Compton, John Alderson, Angela Greene, Paul Stader.

THE BADGE OF MARSHALL BRENNAN (ALLIED ARTISTS) Producer-Director, Albert C. Gannaway; Screenplay by Thomas G. Hubbard; Assistant Director, Lester Guthrie; Music by Ramez Idriss; Song by Hal Levy and Albert Gannaway and Ramez Idriss; Associate Producer, Thomas Hubbard; April release. CAST: Jim Davis, Arleen Whelan, Lee Van Cleef, Louis Jean Heydt, Lawrence Dobkin, Carl Smith, Marty Robbins, Harry Lauter, Douglas Fowley.

GUN DUEL IN DURANGO (UNITED ARTISTS) Producer, Robert E. Kent; Director, Sidney Salkow; Screenplay by Louis Stevens; Music by Paul Sawtell and Bert Shefter; Assistant Director, Ralph E. Black; Wardrobe by Einar Bourman; A Peerless Production; May release. CAST: George Montgomery, Ann Robinson, Steve Brodie, Bobby Clark, Frank Ferguson, Donald Barry, Henry Rowland, Denver Pyle, Mary Treen, Al Wyatt, Red Morgan, Joe Yrigoyen.

THE RIDE BACK (UNITED ARTISTS) Producer, William Conrad; Director, Allen H. Miner; Screenplay by Antony Ellis; Associate Producer, Walter Blake; Music by Frank de Vol; Assistant Director, Robert Justman; Wardrobe by Oscar Rodriguez; Presented by The Associates and Aldrich Company; May release. CAST: Anthony Quinn, William Conrad, George Trevino, Lita Milan, Victor Millan, Ellen Hope Monroe, Joe Dominguez, Louis Towers.

THE LAWLESS EIGHTIES (REPUBLIC) Producer, Rudy Ralston; Director, Joe Kane; Screenplay by Kenneth Gamet; Based on "Brother Van" by Alson Jesse Smith; Assistant Director, Virgil Hart; A Ventura Production in Naturama; May release. CAST: Buster Crabbe, John Smith, Marilyn Saris, Ted de Corsia, Anthony Caruso, John Doucette, Frank Ferguson, Sheila Bromley, Walter Reed, Buzz Henry, Will J. White, Bob Swan.

SIERRA STRANGER (COLUMBIA) Executive Producer, David T. Yokozeki; Producer, Norman T. Herman; Associate Producer, Byron Roberts; Director, Lee Sholem; Story and Screenplay by Richard J. Dorso; Music by Alexander Courage; Assistant Director, Harry R. Sherman; Wardrobe, Tommy Thompson; May release. CAST: Howard Duff, Gloria McGhee, Dick Foran, John Hoyt, Barton MacLane, George E. Stone, Ed Kemmer, Robert Foulk, Eve McVeagh, Henry "Bomber" Kulky, Byron Foulger.

Neville Brand, Jacques Aubuchon, Ruth Donnelly, Walter Brennan, Sheree North, Jeffrey Hunter in "The Way To The Gold"

Walter Reed, Buster Crabbe, Marilyn Saris
in "The Lawless Eighties"

THE WAY TO THE GOLD (20th CENTURY-FOX) Producer, David Weisbart; Director, Robert D. Webb; Screenplay by Wendell Mayes; Based on Novel by Wilbur Daniel Steele; Music by Lionel Newman; Wardrobe, Charles LeMaire; Costumes, Adele Balkan; Assistant Director, Joseph E. Rickards; Songs by Carroll Coates and Lionel Newman; In CinemaScope; May release. CAST: Jeffrey Hunter, Sheree North, Barry Sullivan, Walter Brennan, Neville Brand, Jacques Aubuchon, Ruth Donnelly, Tom Pittman, Philip Ahn, Geraldo Mandia, Ted Edwards, Alan Jeffrey.

BADLANDS OF MONTANA (20th CENTURY-FOX) Produced, Directed and Written by Daniel B. Ullman; Music by Irving Gertz; Song by Gertz and Hal Levy; Sung by Bob Grabeau; A Regal Production; May release. CAST: Rex Reason, Margia Dean, Beverly Garland, Keith Larsen, Emile Meyer, Russ Bender, Robert Cunningham, Ralph Peters, Lee Tung Foo, Stanley Farrar, Rankin Mansfield, William Phipps, John Pickard, Paul Newlan, John Lomma, Jack Kruschen, Elena Da Vinci, George Taylor, William Forester, Larry Blake, Ralph Sanford, William Tanner, Roydon Clark, Helen Jay.

**Derek Farr, Ella Raines, Donald Wolfit
in "The Man In The Road"**

**Barbara Hale, Joel McCrea
in "The Oklahoman"**

THE MAN IN THE ROAD (REPUBLIC) Producer, Charles A. Leeds; Director, Lance Comfort; Screenplay by Guy Morgan; Adapted from Novel "He Was Found In The Road" by Anthony Armstrong; Music by Bruce Campbell; Assistant Director, Frank Hollands; A Gibraltar Production; May release. CAST: Derek Farr, Ella Raines. Donald Wolfit, Lisa Daniely, Karel Stepanek, Cyril Cusack, Olive Sloane, Bruce Beeby. Russell Napier, Frederick Piper, John Welsh, Alfred Maron.

THE WEAPON (REPUBLIC) Producer, Hal E. Chester; Director, Val Guest; Screenplay by Fred Freiberger; Story by Hal E. Chester and Fred Freiberger; Music by James Stevens; Assistant Director, Frank Ernst; May release. CAST: Steve Cochran, Lizabeth Scott, Herbert Marshall, Nicole Maurey, John Whiteley, George Cole, Laurence Naismith, Stanley Maxted, Denis Shaw, Fred Johnson.

THE DEADLY MANTIS (UNIVERSAL) Producer, William Alland; Director, Nathan Juran; Screenplay by Martin Berkeley; Story by William Alland; Gowns by Jay A. Morley, Jr.; Assistant Director, William Holland; May release. CAST: Craig Stevens. William Hopper, Alix Talton, Donald Randolph, Pat Conway, Florenz Ames, Paul Smith, Phil Harvey, Floyd Simmons, Paul Campbell, Helen Jay.

THE OKLAHOMAN (ALLIED ARTISTS) Producer, Walter Mirisch; Associate Producer, Richard Heermance; Director, Francis D. Lyon; Screenplay by Daniel B. Ullman; Assistant Director, Austen Jewell; In CinemaScope and DeLuxe Color; May release. CAST: Joel McCrea, Barbara Hale, Brad Dexter, Gloria Talbott, Verna Felton, Douglas Dick, John Pickard, Michael Pate, Anthony Caruso, Esther Dale, Adam Williams, Ray Teal, Peter Votrian.

CALYPSO JOE (ALLIED ARTISTS) Producer, William F. Broidy; Associate Producer, Lonnie D'Orsa; Director, Edward Dein; Screenplay by Edward and Mildred Dein; Assistant Director, Ralph Slosser; Music by Richard Hazard; Songs by Herb Jeffries and Dick Hazard; May release. CAST: Herb Jeffries, Angie Dickinson, Edward Kemmer, Stephen Bekassy, Laurie Mitchell, Robert Sherman, Claudia Drake, Murray Alper, Linda Terrace, Charles R. Keans, Lord Flea, The Easy Riders, The Lester Horton Dancers, Duke of Iron.

HOT ROD RUMBLE (ALLIED ARTISTS) Producer, Norman Herman; Director, Les Martinson; Screenplay by Meyer Dolinsky; Assistant Director, Paul Wurtzel; A Nacirema Production; May release. CAST: Leigh Snowden, Richard Hartunian, Brett Halsey. Wright King, Joey Forman, Larry Dolgin, John Brinkley, Chuck Webster, Ned Glass, Phil Adams, Joe Mell.

**Aram Katcher, Zsa Zsa Gabor, Lex Barker,
Maurice Manson in "The Girl In The Kremlin"**

**Ross Allen, Dottie Lee Phillips
in "Deep Adventure"**

THE GIRL IN THE KREMLIN (UNIVERSAL) Producer, Albert Zugsmith; Director, Russell Birdwell; Screenplay by Gene L. Coon and Robert Hill; Based on Story by Harry Ruskin and DeWitt Bodeen; Gowns by Bill Thomas; Assistant Director, Marshall Green; May release. CAST: Lex Barker, Zsa Zsa Gabor, Jeffrey Stone, Maurice Manson, Natalia Daryll, William Schallert, Aram Katcher, Norbert Schiller, Michael Fox, Elena Davinci, Phillipa Fallon, Charles Horvath, Kurt Katch, Vanda Dupre, Alfred Linder, Gabor Curtiz, Della Maltzahn.

DEEP ADVENTURE (WARNER BROS.) Producer, Cedric Francis; Director, Charles Welborn; Screenplay by Owen Crump; Music by 'Howard Jackson; May release. CAST: Ross Allen, William Fuller. Dottie Lee Phillips.

SHOOT-OUT AT MEDICINE BEND (WARNER BROS.) Producer, Richard Whorf; Director, Richard L. Bare; Screenplay by John Tucker Battle and D. D. Beauchamp; Music by Roy Webb; Song by Ray Heindorf and Wayne Shanklin; Costumes by Marjorie Best; Assistant Director, William Kissell; May release. CAST: Randolph Scott, James Craig, Angie Dickinson, Dani Crayne, James Garner, Gordon Jones, Trevor Bardette, Don Beddoe, Myron Healey, John Alderson, Harry Harvey, Sr., Robert Warwick.

Gordon Jones, Randolph Scott, James Garner
in "Shoot-Out At Medicine Bend"

John Beal, Kenneth Tobey
in "The Vampire"

LURE OF THE SWAMP (20th CENTURY-FOX)
Producer, Sam Hersh; Director. Hubert Cornfield;
Screenplay by William George from Novel by Gil
Brewer; Music by Paul Dunlap; A Regalscope
Film; May release. CAST: Marshall Thompson,
Willard Parker, Joan Vohs, Jack Elam, Joan Lora,
James Maloney, Leo Gordon.

THE RESTLESS BREED (20th CENTURY-FOX)
Producer, Edward L. Alperson; Director, Allan
Dwan; Screenplay by Steve Fisher; Music by
Edward L. Alperson, Jr.; Songs by Dick Hughes
and Richard Stapley and Edward L. Alperson, Jr.;
In Eastman Color; May release. CAST: Scott
Brady, Anne Bancroft, Jay C. Flippen, Rhys
Williams, Jim Davis, Leo Gordon, Scott Marlowe,
Eddy Waller, Harry Cheshire, Myron Healey,
Gerald Milton, Dennis King, Jr., James Flavan.

UNTAMED YOUTH (WARNER BROS.) Producer,
Aubrey Schenck; Director, Howard W. Koch;
Screenplay by John C. Higgins; Story by Stephen
Longstreet; Music by Les Baxter; Songs by Les
Baxter and Lenny Adelson; Assistant Director,
Tommy Thompson; May release. CAST: Mamie
Van Doren, Lori Nelson, John Russell, Don Burnett,
Eddie Cochran, Lurene Tuttle, Yvonne Lime,
Jeanne Carmen, Robert Foulk, Wayne Taylor,
Jerry Barclay, Keith Richards, Valerie Reynolds,
Lucita, Glenn Dixon, Wally Brown.

THE UNEARTHLY (REPUBLIC) Producer-Di-
rector, Brooke L. Peters; an AB-PT Picture; June
release. CAST: John Carradine, Allison Hayes,
Myron Healy, Sally Todd, Marilyn Buferd, Arthur
Batanides, Tor Johnson, Harry Fleer, Roy Gordon,
Guy Prescott, Paul MacWilliams.

TWO GROOMS FOR A BRIDE (20th CENTURY-
FOX) Producers, Robert S. Baker and Monty
Berman; Director. Henry Cass; Screenplay by
Frederick Stephani; Music by Stanley Black; An
Eros Film; June release. CAST: John Carroll,
Virginia Bruce, Brian Oulton, Kay Callard, Michael
Caridia, Barbara Brown, Kit Terrington, Alexander
Gauge, Donald Stewart, Anita Sharp Bolster,
Arthur Lowe, Tim Gill, Earnest Jay, Michael
Balfour, Karen Greer, Tucker Maguire, Ann Doran.

THE VAMPIRE (UNITED ARTISTS) Producers,
Arthur Gardner and Jules V. Levy; Director, Paul
Landres; Story and Screenplay by Pat Fielder;
Assistant Director. Marty Moss; Associate Producer,
Arnold Laven; Music by Gerald Fried; June
release. CAST: John Beal, Coleen Gray, Kenneth
Tobey, Lydia Reed, Dabbs Greer, Herb Vigran,
Paul Brinegar, Ann Staunton, James Griffith,
Natalie Masters, Louise Lewis, Wood Romoff, Brad
Morrow, Hallene Hill, Raymond Greenleaf, Mauritz
Hugo, Anne O'Neal, George Selk, Walter A.
Merrill, Christine Rees, Arthur Gardner.

Anne Bancroft, Scott Brady
in "The Restless Breed"

Barbara Stanwyck, Joel McCrea
in "Trooper Hook"

CHINA GATE (20th CENTURY-FOX) Produced,
Directed and Written by Samuel Fuller; Music by
Victor Young and Max Steiner; In CinemaScope;
May release. CAST: Gene Barry, Nat "King"
Cole, Angie Dickinson, Paul Dubov, Lee Van
Cleef, George Givot, Gerald Milton, Neyle Morrow,
Marcel Dalio, Maurice Marsac, Warren Hsieh,
Paul Busch, Sasha Harden, James Hong, William
Soo Hoo, Walter Soo Hoo, Weaver Levy.

THE COUNTERFEIT PLAN (WARNER BROS.)
Producer, Alec C. Snowden; Director, Montgomery
Tully; Screenplay by James Eastwood; Assistant
Director, Bill Shore; An Amalgamated Production;
May release. CAST: Zachary Scott, Peggie Castle,
Mervyn Johns, Sydney Tafler, Lee Patterson, David
Lodge, Mark Bellamy, Chili Bouchier, Robert
Arden, Eric Pohlmann, Aubrey Dexter, John Welsh.

TROOPER HOOK (UNITED ARTISTS) Producer,
Sol Baer Fielding; Director, Charles Marquis War-
ren; Screenplay by Charles Marquis Warren, David
Victor and Herbert Little Jr.; Based on Story by
Jack Schaefer; Music by Gerald Fried; Assistant
Directors, Nathan Barragar and Nat Holt, Jr.; June
release. CAST: Joel McCrea, Barbara Stanwyck,
Earl Holliman, Edward Andrews, John Dehner,
Susan Kohner, Royal Dano, Terry Lawrence, Celia
Lovsky, Rudolfo Acosta, Stanley Adams, Pat
O'Moore, Jeanne Bates, Rush Williams, Dick
Shannon, D. J. Thompson, Sheb Wooley, Cyril
Delivanti.

James Craig, Kristine Miller, William Talman,
Georgia Lee, Darryl Hickman, Alvy Moore in
"The Persuader"

Gia Scala, Kerwin Mathews
in "The Garment Jungle"

THE PERSUADER (ALLIED ARTISTS) Producer-
Director, Dick Ross; Associate Producer, James F.
Collier; Screenplay by Curtis Kenyon; Assistant
Director, Dolph Zimmer; Music by Ralph Car-
michael; Song by Ralph Carmichael; Sung by
James Joyce; A World Wide Picture; June release.
CAST: William Talman, James Craig, Kristine
Miller, Darryl Hickman, Georgia Lee, Alvy Moore,
Gregory Walcott, Rhoda Williams, Paul Engle,
Jason Johnson, Nolan Leary, John Milford, Frank
Richards.

THE GARMENT JUNGLE (COLUMBIA) Producer,
Harry Kleiner; Director. Vincent Sherman; Story
and Screenplay by Harry Kleiner from Articles by
Lester Velie; Gowns by Jean Louis; Music by Leith
Stevens; Assistant Director. Irving Moore; June
release. CAST: Lee J. Cobb, Kerwin Mathews,
Gia Scala, Richard Boone, Valerie French, Robert
Loggia, Joseph Wiseman, Harold J. Stone, Adam
Williams, Wesley Addy, Willis Bouchey, Robert
Ellenstein, Celia Lovsky.

DESTINATION 60,000 (ALLIED ARTISTS) Pro-
ducers, Jack J. Gross and Philip N. Krasne;
Directed and written by George Waggner; As-
sistant Director, Hal Klein; Music by Al Glasser;
June release. CAST: Preston Foster, Pat Conway,
Jeff Donnell, Coleen Gray, Bobby Clark, Denver
Pyle, Russ Thorson, Ann Barton.

JOURNEY TO FREEDOM (REPUBLIC) Producer,
Stephen C. Apostolof; Director, Robert C. Dertano;
Screenplay by Herbert F. Niccolls; Story by
Stephen C. Apostolof and Herbert F. Niccolls;
Associate Producer, Stafford B. Harrison; Music
by Josef Zimanich; June release. CAST: Jacques
Scott, Geneviv Aumont, George Graham, Morgan
Lane, Jean Ann Lewis, Peter E. Besbas, Don
McArt, Dan O'Dowd, Barry O'Hara, Fred Kohler,
Tor Johnson, Don Marlowe, Miles Shepard.

BEGINNING OF THE END (REPUBLIC) Pro-
ducer-Director, Bert I. Gordon; Screenplay by
Fred Freiberger and Lester Gorn; An AB-PT
Production; June release. CAST: Peggie Castle,
Peter Graves, Morris Ankrum, Richard Benedict,
James Seay, Thomas B. Henry, Than Wynnn, John
Close, Don C. Harvey, Larry J. Blake, Pierre
Watkin, Steve Warren, Frank Conner, Don Eitner,
Frank Chase, Frank Wilcox, Alan Reynolds, Alan
Wells, Eilene Janssen, Hylton Socher, Patricia
Dean, Paul Grant.

BAYOU (UNITED ARTISTS) Executive Producer,
M. A. Ripps; Director, Harold Daniels; Story and
Screenplay by Edward I. Fessler; Songs by Edward
I. Fessler; June release. CAST: Peter Graves,
Lita Milan, Douglas Fowley, Tim Carey, Jonathan
Haze, Edwin Nelson, Eugene Sondfield, Evelyn
Hendrickson, Milton Schneider, Michael R. Romano.

Jeff Donnell, Preston Foster, Bobby Clark
in "Destination 60,000"

Peter Graves, Lita Milan
in "Bayou"

THE MONSTER THAT CHANGED THE WORLD
(UNITED ARTISTS) Producers, Jules V. Levy and
Arthur Gardner; Director, Arnold Laven; Screen-
play by Pat Fielder; Story by David Duncan;
Assistant Director, Maurice Vaccarino; Music by
Heinz Roemheld; June release. CAST: Tim Holt,
Audrey Dalton, Hans Conreid, Harlan Ware,
Casey Adams, Mimi Gibson, Gordon Jones, Marjorie
Stapp, Dennis McCarthy, Barbara Darrow, Bob
Beneveds, Michael Dugan, Mack Williams, Eileen
Harley, Jody McCrea, William Swan, Charles Tan-
nen, Byron Kane, Hal Taggert, Gil Frye Dan
Gachman, Milton Parsons, Ralph Moody.

INVASION OF THE SAUCER MEN (AMERICAN-
INTERNATIONAL) Producers, James H. Nicholson
and Robert J. Gurney, Jr.; Executive Producer,
Samuel Z. Arkoff; Director, Edward L. Cahn;
Story by Paul Fairman; Screenplay by Robert J.
Gurney, Jr. and Al Martin; Music by Ronald
Stein; A Malibu Production; June release. CAST:
Steve Terrell, Gloria Castillo, Frank Gorshin,
Raymond Hatton, Lyn Osborn, Russ Bender,
Douglas Henderson, Sam Buffington, Jason Johnson,
Don Shelton, Scott Peters, Jan Englund, Kelly
Thordsen, Bob Einer, Patti Lawler, Calvin Booth,
Ed Nelson, Roy Darmour, Audrey Conti, Jim
Bridges, Jimmy Pickford, Joan Dupuis, Buddy
Mason, Orv Mohler, Angelo Rossito, Floyd Dixon,
Dean Neville, Edward Peter Gibbons.

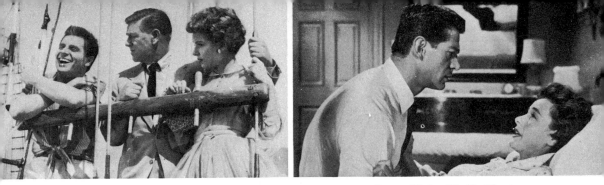

Johnny Desmond, Paul Langton, Merry Anders in "Calypso Heat Wave"

George Nader, Phyllis Thaxter in "Man Afraid"

CALYPSO HEAT WAVE (COLUMBIA) Producer, Sam Katzman; Director. Fred F. Sears; Screenplay by David Chandler; Story by Orville H. Hampton; Assistant Director, Leonard Katzman; Dances Staged and Created by Josephine Earl; A Clover Production; June release. CAST: Johnny Desmond, Merry Anders, Meg Myles, Paul Langton, Joel Grey, Michael Granger, George E. Stone, The Treniers, The Tarriers, The Hi-Lo's, Maya Angelou, Dick Whittinghill, Darla Hood, Pierce Lyden, Gil Perkins, William Challee, Mac Niles and The Calypsonians.

THE NIGHT THE WORLD EXPLODED (COLUMBIA) Producer, Sam Katzman; Director, Fred F. Sears; Screenplay by Jack Natteford and Luci Ward; Assistant Director, Willard Sheldon; A Clover Production; June release. CAST: Kathryn Grant, William Leslie, Tris Coffin, Raymond Greenleaf, Charles Evans, Frank Scannell, Marshall Reed, Fred Coby, Paul Savage, Terry Frost.

THE GIANT CLAW (COLUMBIA) Producer, Sam Katzman; Director, Fred F. Sears; Screenplay by Samuel Newman and Paul Gangelin; Assistant Director, Leonard Katzman; A Clover Production; June release. CAST: Jeff Morrow, Mara Corday, Morris Ankrum, Louis D. Merrill, Edgar Barrier, Robert Shayne, Ruell Shayne, Clark Howat, Morgan Jones.

MAN AFRAID (UNIVERSAL) Producer, Gordon Kay; Director, Harry Keller; Screenplay by Herb Meadow; Story by Dan Ullman; Gowns, Bill Thomas; Assistant Director, Frank Shaw; Music by Henry Mancini; June release. CAST: George Nader, Phyllis Thaxter, Tim Hovey, Eduard Franz, Harold J. Stone, Judson Pratt. Reta Shaw, Butch Bernard, Mabel Albertson, Martin Milner.

THE BIG CAPER (UNITED ARTISTS) Producers, William C. Thomas and Howard Pine; Director, Robert Stevens; Screenplay by Martin Berkeley; Based on Novel by Lionel White; Assistant Director, Frank Fox; Music by Albert Glasser; June release. CAST: Rory Calhoun, Mary Costa, James Gregory, Robert Harris, Corey Allen, Roxanne Arlen, Paul Picerni, Pat McVey, James Nolan, Florenz Ames, Louise Arthur, Roscoe Ates, Terry Kelman, Melody Gale.

BEYOND MOMBASA (COLUMBIA) Producer, Tony Owen; Director, George Marshall; Screenplay by Richard English and Gene Levitt; Based on Story "The Mark of The Leopard" by James Eastwood; Music by Humphrey Searle; Assistant Director, Basil Keys; A Todon Production in Technicolor; June release. CAST: Cornel Wilde, Donna Reed, Leo Genn, Ron Randell, Christopher Lee, Eddie Calvert, Dan Jackson, MacDonald Parke, Virginia Bedard, Julian Sherrier, Edward Johnson, Bartholomew Sketch.

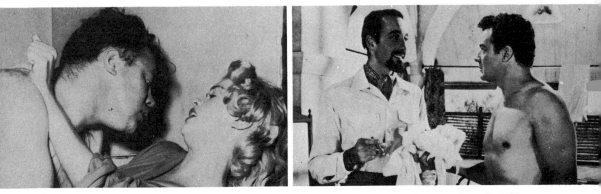

Mickey Shaughnessy, Jayne Mansfield in "The Burglar"

Christopher Lee, Cornel Wilde in "Beyond Mombasa"

THE BURGLAR (COLUMBIA) Producer, Louis W. Kellman; Director, Paul Wendkos; Screenplay by David Goodis; Adapted from his Novel; Music by Sol Kaplan; Song by Bob Marcucchi and Pete de Angelo; Sung by Vince Carson; June release. CAST: Dan Duryea, Jayne Mansfield, Matha Vickers, Peter Capell, Mickey Shaughnessy, Wendell Phillips, Phoebe Mackay, Steward Bradley. Frank Orrison, Sam Elber, Ned Carey, John Boyd, Michael Kane, George Kane. Sam Cresson, Ruth Burnat, John Facenda, Frank Hall, Steve Allison, Richard Emery, Andrea McLaughlin.

I WAS A TEENAGE WEREWOLF (AMERICAN-INTERNATIONAL) Producer, Herman Cohen; Director. Gene Fowler, Jr.; Story and Screenplay by Ralph Thornton; Assistant Director, Jack R. Berne; Music by Paul Dunlap; Song by Jerry Blaine; June release. CAST: Michael Landon, Yvonne Lime, Whit Bissell, Tony Marshall, Dawn Richard, Barney Phillips, Ken Miller, Cindy Robbins, Michael Rougas, Robert Griffin, Joseph Mell, Malcom Atterbury, Eddie Marr Vladimir Sokoloff, Louise Lewis, John Launer, Guy Williams, Dorothy Crehan.

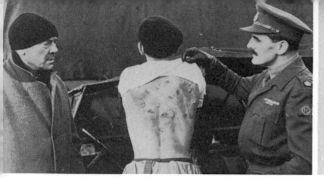

Dean Jagger, John Harvey
in "X The Unknown"

Keith Larsen, Jim Davis
in "Apache Warrior"

SPOOK CHASERS (ALLIED ARTISTS) Producer, Ben Schwalb; Director, George Blair; Assistant Directors, Austen Jewell and Lindsley Parsons, Jr.; June release. CAST: Huntz Hall, Stanley Clements, Percy Helton, Jimmy Murphy. David Condon, Eddie LeRoy, Bill Henry, Darlene Fields, Peter Mamakos, Ben Welden, Robert Christopher, Pierre Watkin.

20 MILLION MILES TO EARTH (COLUMBIA) Producer, Charles H. Schneer; Director, Nathan Juran; Screenplay by Bob Williams and Christopher Knopf; Story by Charlott Knight and Ray Harryhausen; Assistant Director, Eddie Saeta and Octavio Oppo; A Morningside Production; July release. CAST: William Hopper, Joan Taylor, Frank Puglia, John Zaremba, Thomas B. Henry, Tito Vuolo, Jan Arvan, Arthur Space, Bart Bradley, George Pelling, George Khoury, Don Orlando, Rollin Moriyama.

X THE UNKNOWN (WARNER BROS.) Producer, Anthony Hinds; Director, Leslie Norman; Story and Screenplay by Jimmy Sangster; Music by James Bernard; Assistant Director, Chris Sutton; July release. CAST: Dean Jagger, Edward Chapman, Leo McKern, William Lucas, John Harvey, Peter Hammond, Michael Ripper, Anthony Newley; Ian MacNaughton, Kenneth Cope, Marianne Brauns.

LAST STAGECOACH WEST (REPUBLIC) Producer, Rudy Ralston; Director, Joe Kane; Screenplay by Barry Shipman; Assistant Director, Virgil Hart; A Ventura Production in Naturama; July release. CAST: Jim Davis, Mary Castle, Victor Jory, Lee Van Cleef, Grant Withers, Roy Barcroft, John Alderson, Glenn Strange, Francis McDonald, Willis Bouchey, Lewis Martin, Tristram Coffin.

APACHE WARRIOR (20th CENTURY-FOX) Producer, Plato Skouras; Director, Elmo Williams; Screenplay by Carroll Young, Kurt Neumann and Eric Norden; Music by Paul Dunlap; A Regalscope Film; July release. CAST: Keith Larsen, Jim Davis, Rodolfo Acosta, John Miljan, Eddie Little, Michael Carr, George Keymas, Lane Bradford, Eugenia Paul, Damian O'Flynn, Dehl Berti, Nick Thompson, Ray Kellogg, Allan Nixon, Karl Davis, David Carlisle.

THE 27th DAY (COLUMBIA) Producer, Helen Ainsworth; Executive Producer, Lewis J. Rachmil; Director, William Asher; Screenplay by John Mantley based on his Novel; Assistant Director, Willard Sheldon; A Romson Production; July release. CAST: Gene Barry. Valerie French, George Voskovec, Arnold Moss, Stefan Schnabel, Ralph Clanton, Frederick Ledebur. Paul Birch, Azemat Janti, Marie Tsien, Ed Hinton, Grandon Rhodes.

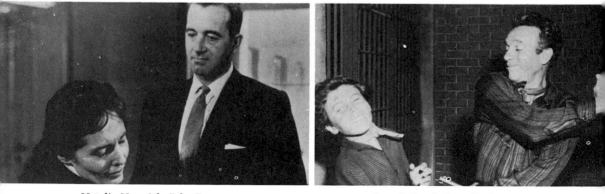

Natalie Norwick, John Payne
in "Hidden Fear"

Joseph "Bucko" Stafford, Dane Clark
in "Outlaw's Son"

HIDDEN FEAR (UNITED ARTISTS) Producers, Robert St. Aubrey and Howard E. Kohn II; Director, Andre de Toth; Story and Screenplay by Andre de Toth and John Ward Hawkins; Assistant Directors, Jesper Gottschalch, Ole Mynster, Asger Jerrild and Karen Petersen; Music by Hans Schreiber; Costumes by Magasin du Nord; July release. CAST: John Payne, Alexander Knox, Conrad Nagel, Natalie Norwick, Anne Neyland, Kjeld Jacobsen, Paul Erling, Mogens Brandt, Marianne Schleiss, Knud Rex, Elsie Albiin, Buster Larsen, Kjeld Petersen, Preben Mahrt.

OUTLAW'S SON (UNITED ARTISTS) Executive Producer, Aubrey Schenck; Producer, Howard W. Koch; Director, Lesley Selander; Screenplay by Richard Alan Simmons; Based on "Gambling Man" by Clifton Adams; Music by Les Baxter; Assistant Director, Austen Jewell; A Bel-Air Production; July release. CAST: Dane Clark, Ben Cooper, Lori Nelson, Ellen Drew, Charles Watts, Cecile Rogers, Joseph "Bucko" Stafford, Eddie Foy III, John Pickard, Robert Knapp, Les Mitchel, Guy Prescott, George Pembroke, Jeff Daley, Wendy Stuart, Anna Maria Nanasi, James Parnell, Scott Peters, Buddy Hart, Ernie Dotson, Ken Christy, Audley Anderson, Leslie Kimmell.

**Tom Drake, Lon Chaney, Jr., James Craig
in "Cyclops"**

**Robert Christopher, Allison Hayes, Paul Burke
in "The Disembodied"**

GOD IS MY PARTNER (20th CENTURY-FOX) Producer, Sam Hersh; Director, William F. Claxton; Screenplay by Charles Francis Royal; Music by Paul Dunlap; A Regalscope Film; July release. CAST: Walter Brennan, John Hoyt, Marion Ross, Jesse White, Nelson Leigh, Charles Lane, Ellen Corby, Paul Cavanagh, Nancy Kulp, John Harmon.

THE DISEMBODIED (ALLIED ARTISTS) Producer, Ben Schwalb; Director, Walter Grauman; Screenplay by Jack Townley; Assistant Director, Austen Jewell; Music by Marlin Skiles; July release. CAST: Paul Burke, Allison Hayes, John E. Wengraf, Eugenia Paul, Joel Marston, Robert Christopher, Norman Fredric, A. E. Ukonu, Paul Thompson, Otis Greene.

CYCLOPS (ALLIED ARTISTS) Produced, Directed and Written by Bert I. Gordon; Associate Producer, Henry Schrage; Assistant Producer, Flora M. Gordon; Assistant Directors, Harry O. Jones and Ray Taylor, Jr.; Music by Albert Glasser; A B & H Production; July release. CAST: James Craig, Gloria Talbott, Lon Chaney, Jr., Tom Drake.

DAUGHTER OF DR. JEKYLL (ALLIED ARTISTS) Produced and Written by Jack Pollexfen; Associate Producer, Ilse Lahn; July release. CAST: John Agar, Gloria Talbott, Arthur Shields, John Dierkes, Martha Wentworth, Mollie McCart.

BOP GIRL (UNITED ARTISTS) Producer, Aubrey Schenck; Director, Howard W. Koch; Screenplay by Arnold Belgard; Story by Henrik Vollaerts; Music by Les Baxter; Assistant Director, Paul Wurtzel; Clothes by Paul Giokaris; A Bel-Air Production; July release. CAST: Judy Tyler, Bobby Troup, Margo Woode, Lucien Littlefield, George O'Hanlon, Jerry Barclay, Judy Harriet, Gene O'Donnell, Edward Kafafian, George Sawaya, Jerry Frank, Dick Standish, Mary Kaye Trio, The Goofers, Lord Flea and His Calypsonians, Nino Tempo, The Titans, The Cubanos.

THE LAND UNKNOWN (UNIVERSAL) Producer, William Alland; Director, Virgil Vogel; Screenplay by Laszlo Gorog; Story by Charles Palmer; Adaptation by William N. Robson; Assistant Director, Joseph E. Kenny; In CinemaScope; August release. CAST: Jock Mahoney, Shawn Smith, William Reynolds, Henry Brandon, Phil Harvey, Douglas Kennedy.

NAKED AFRICA (AMERICAN-INTERNATIONAL) Produced and Directed by Cedric Worth; Directed and Photographed by Ray Phoenix; Associate Producer, Morrie Roizman; Narrated by Quentin Reynolds; A Jaywall Production; August release. A Documentary about Africa's wild life and people and the effect the outside world has had on both of them.

**Shawn Smith, William Reynolds, Phil Harvey,
Jock Mahoney in "The Land Unknown"**

**Patricia Medina, Richard Denning
in "The Buckskin Lady"**

THE CURSE OF FRANKENSTEIN (WARNER BROS.) Producer, Anthony Hinds; Director, Terrence Fisher; Associate Producer, Anthony Nelson-Keys; Screenplay by Jimmy Sangster; Based on Story by Mary W. Shelley; Assistant Director, Derek Whitehurst; Executive Producer, Michael Carreras; Music by James Bernard; A Hammer Production; July release. CAST: Peter Cushing, Hazel Court, Robert Urquhart, Christopher Lee, Valerie Gaunt, Melvyn Hayes, Paul Hardtmuth, Fred Johnson, Noel Hood, Alex Gallier. Michael Mulcaster, Claude Kingston, Andrew Leigh, Ann Blake, Sally Walsh, Middleton Woods, Raymond Ray.

THE BUCKSKIN LADY (UNITED ARTISTS) Producer-Director, Carl K. Hittleman; Screenplay by David Lang and Carl K. Hittleman; Story by Francis S. Chase, Jr.; Associate Producer, D. Jersey Grut; Music by Albert Glasser; Song by Albert Glasser and Maurice Keller; Assistant Director, Ray Heinze; July release. CAST: Patricia Medina, Richard Denning, Gerald Mohr, Henry Hull, Hank Warden, Robin Short, Richard Reeves, Dorothy Adams, Frank Sully, George Cisar, Louis Lettieri, Byron Foulger, John Dierkes.

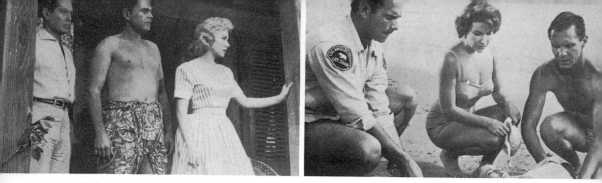

Tod Andrews, Tina Carver
in "From Hell It Came"

Dan Seymour, Mara Corday
in "Undersea Girl"

WHITE HUNTRESS (AMERICAN-INTERNA-
TIONAL) Producers, John Croydon and Peter
Crane; Director, George Breakston; Screenplay
by Dermot Quinn; Assistant Director, Robert
Foster; Music by Philip Green; August release.
CAST: Susan Stephan, John Bently, Robert
Urquhart.

FROM HELL IT CAME (ALLIED ARTISTS)
Producer, Jack Milner; Associate Producers, Richard
Bernstein and Byron Roberts; Director, Dan Milner;
Screenplay by Richard Lernstein; Story by Richard
Bernstein and Jack Milner; Assistant Director,
Johnny Greenwald; Music by Darrell Calker;
August release. CAST: Tod Andrews, Tina Carver,
Linda Watkins, Jchn McNamara, Gregg Palmer,
Robert Swan, Baynes Barron, Suzanne Ridgway,
Mark Sheeler, Lee Rhodes, Grace Matthews, Tani
Marsh, Chester Hayes, Lenmana Guerin.

PORTLAND EXPOSE (ALLIED ARTISTS) Pro-
ducer, Lindsley Parsons; Associate Producer, John
H. Burrows; Director, Harold Schuster; Screenplay
by Jack DeWitt; Assistant Director, Lindsley
Parsons, Jr.; Music by Paul Dunlap; August release.
CAST: Edward Binns, Carolyn Craig, Virginia
Gregg, Russ Conway, Larry Dobkin, Frank Gorshin,
Joe Marr, Rusty Lane, Dickie Bellis, Lea Penman,
Jeanne Carmen, Stanley Farrar, Larry Thor, Francis
de Sales, Kort Falkenberg, Joe Flynn.

NO TIME TO BE YOUNG (COLUMBIA) Producer,
Wallace MacDonald; Director, David Rich; Screen-
play by John McPartland and Raphael Hayes;
Story by John McPartland; Assistant Director,
Charles S. Gould; August release. CAST: Robert
Vaughn, Roger Smith, Tom Pittman, Dorothy Green,
Merry Anders, Kathy Nolan, Sarah Selby, Fred
Sherman, Ralph Clanton, Don C. Harvey, Bonnie
Bolding.

UNDERSEA GIRL (ALLIED ARTISTS) Executive
Producer, David T. Yokozeki; Producer, Norman
T. Herman; Director, John Peyser; Assistant Di-
rector, Hal Klein; A Nacirema Production; August
release. CAST: Pat Conway, Mara Corday, Dan
Seymour, Florence Marly, Ralph Clanton, Myron
Healy, Lewis Charles, Jerry Eskow, Dehl Berti,
Brick Sullivan, Sue George, Mickey Simpson, Mike
Mason, Don Warren, Jess Kirkpatrick, Russ Thorsen,
Corrine Laine, William Kendis, Mack Chandler.

VALERIE (UNITED ARTISTS) Producer, Hal R.
Makelim; Director, Gerd Oswald; Screenplay by
Leonard Heideman and Emmett Murphy; August
release. CAST: Sterling Hayden, Anita Ekberg,
Anthony Steel, Peter Walker, John Wengraf,
Iphigenie Castiglioni, Jerry Barclay, Robert Adler,
Tom McKee, Gage Clarke, Sidney Smith, Norman
Leavitt, Juney Ellis, Malcolm Atterbury, Stanley
Adams, Brian O'Hara, John Dierkes.

Rex Ingram, Helmut Dantine
in "Hell On Devil's Island"

Fay Compton, Alec McCowen
in "Town On Trial"

HELL ON DEVIL'S ISLAND (20th CENTURY-
FOX) Producers, Leon Chooluck and Lawrence
Stewart; Director, Christian Nyby; Screenplay by
Steven Ritch; Music by Irving Gertz; Based on
Story by Arndt and Ethel Giusti; August release.
CAST: Helmut Dantine, William Talman, Donna
Martell, Jean Willes, Rex Ingram, Robert Cornth-
waite, Jav Adler, Peter Adams, Edward Colmans,
Mel Welles, Charles Bohbot, Alan Lee, Henry
Rowland, Edward Coch, Paul Brinegar, Allen
Pinson, Roy Jenson, Elena Da Vinci, Edwin Nelson,
Paul MacWilliams.

TOWN ON TRIAL (COLUMBIA) Producer, Max-
well Setton; Director, John Guillermin; Screenplay
by Robert Westerby and Ken Hughes; Associate
Producer, William Weedon; Assistant Director,
Fred Slark; Music by Tristram Cary; Dance Music
by Paul Brousse; August release. CAST: Charles
Coburn, Barbara Bates, John Mills, Derek Farr,
Alec McCowen, Fay Compton, Geoffrey Keen,
Margaretta Scott, Meredith Edwards, Harry Locke,
Raymond Huntley, Harry Fowler, Elizabeth Seal,
Maureen Connell, Magda Miller, Newton Blick,
Oscar Quitak, Trottie Truman Taylor, Grace
Arnold.

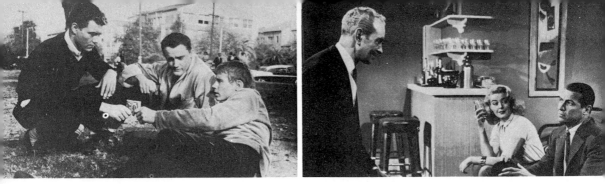

**Roger Smith, Robert Vaughn, Tom Pittman
in "No Time To Be Young"**

**Robert Bray (Right)
in "My Gun Is Quick"**

JUNGLE HEAT (UNITED ARTISTS) Executive Producer, Aubrey Schenck; Director, Howard W. Koch; Screenplay by Jameson Brewer; Music by Les Baxter; Assistant Director, Henry E. Brill; A Bel-Air Production; August release. CAST: Lex Barker, Mari Blanchard, Glenn Langan, James Westerfield, Rhodes Reason, Miyoko Sasaki, Glenn Dixon, Bob Okazaki, Jerry Frank, Daniel Wong, Andrew Gross, Yun Kui Chang, Kunio Fudimura, Leo Ezell.

LADY OF VENGEANCE (UNITED ARTISTS) Producers, Burt Balaban and Bernard Donnenfeld; Director, Burt Balaban; Story and Screenplay by Irve Tunick; Music by Phil Cardew; Assistant Director, Percy Hermes; August release. CAST: Dennis O'Keefe, Ann Sears, Anton Diffring, Patrick Barr, Vernon Greeves, Eileen Elton, Frederick Schiller, Jacqueline Curtiss, George Mulcaster, Gerald Case, Jack McNaughton, Colin Croft, Andy Ho, Humphrey Morton.

ROCK AROUND THE WORLD (AMERICAN-INTERNATIONAL) Producers, Peter Rogers and Herbert Smith; Director, Gerard Bryant; August release. CAST: Tommy Steele, Nancy Whiskey, Hunter Hancock, The Steelmen, Humphrey Lyttelton and His Band, Chris O'Brien's Carribeans, Tommy Eytle's Calypso Band, Charles McDevitt's Skiffle Group.

MY GUN IS QUICK (UNITED ARTISTS) Produced and Directed by George A. White and Phil Victor; Screenplay by Richard Collins and Richard Powell; Story by Richard Powell; Based on Novel by Mickey Spillane; Music by Marlin Skiles; August release. CAST: Robert Bray, Whitney Blake, Pat Donahue, Donald Randolph, Pamela Duncan, Booth Colman, Jan Chaney, Virginia Core, Richard Garland, Charles Boaz, Peter Mamakos, Claire Carleton, Phil Arnold, John Dennis, Terrence De Marney, Jackie Paul, Leon Askin.

TAMING SUTTON'S GAL (REPUBLIC) Producer, William J. O'Sullivan; Director, Lesley Selander; Screenplay by Thames Williamson and Frederic Louis Fox; Story by Thames Williamson; Assistant Director, Leonard Kunody; A Variety Production in Naturama; September release. CAST: John Lupton, Gloria Talbott, Jack Kelly, May Wynn, Verna Felton.

THE WAYWARD GIRL (REPUBLIC) Producer, William J. O'Sullivan; Director, Lesley Selander; Screenplay by Houston Branch and Frederic Louis Fox; Assistant Director, Leonard Kunody; A Variety Production in Naturama; September release. CAST: Marcia Henderson, Peter Walker, Katharine Barrett, Whit Bissell, Rita Lynn, Peg Hillias, Tracey Roberts, Ray Teal, Ric Roman, Barbara Eden, Grandon Rhodes, Francis DeSales, John Maxwell.

**Anita Ekberg, Anthony Steel
in "Valerie"**

**Tommy Steele (Right)
in "Rock Around The World"**

REFORM SCHOOL GIRL (AMERICAN-INTERNATIONAL) Producers, Robert J. Gurney, Jr. and Samuel Z. Arkoff; Direction and Screenplay by Edward Bernds; Music by Ronald Stein; A Carmel Production; August release. CAST: Gloria Castillo, Ross Ford, Edward Byrnes, Ralph Reed, Jan Englund, Yvette Vickers, Helen Wallace, Donna Jo Gribble, Luana Anders, Diana Darrin, Nesdon Booth, Wayne Taylor, Sharon Lee, Jack Kruschen, Linda Rivera, Elaine Sinclair, Dorothy Crehan, Claire Carleton, Lillian Powell, Sally Kellerman.

PAWNEE (REPUBLIC) Producers, Jack J. Gross and Philip N. Krasne; Director, George Waggner; Screenplay by George Waggner, Louis Vittes, Endre Bohem; Music by Paul Sawtell; Associate Producer, Sol Dolgin; Assistant Director, Hal Klein; In Trucolor; September release. CAST: George Montgomery, Bill Williams, Lola Albright, Francis J. McDonald, Robert E. Griffin, Dabbs Greer, Kathleen Freeman, Charlotte Austin, Ralph Moody, Anne Barton, Raymond Hatton, Charles Horvath, Robert Nash.

173

Jock Mahoney, Anthony Caruso, Claude Akins
in "Joe Dakota"

Brian Keith, Beverly Garland, Paul Langton
in "Chicago Confidential"

THE CAT GIRL (AMERICAN-INTERNATIONAL)
Producers, Lou Rusoff and Herbert Smith; Executive
Producer, Peter Rogers; Directors, Peter Hennessy
and Alfred Shaughnessy; Screenplay by Lou Rusoff;
A Malibu Production. September release. CAST:
Barbara Shelley, Robert Ayres, Kay Callard, Paddy
Webster, Ernest Milton, Lilly Kann, Jack May,
John Lee, Martin Body, John Watson, Selma Vaz
Dias, John Baker, Frank Atkinson, Geoffery
Tyrrell.

JOE DAKOTA (UNIVERSAL) Producer, Howard
Christie; Director, Richard Bartlett; Screenplay by
William Talman and Norman Jolley; Gowns by
Marilyn Sotto; Assistant Director, Frank Shaw;
Song by Mack David and Ray Joseph; September
release. CAST: Jock Mahoney, Luana Patten,
Charles McGraw, Barbara Lawrence, Claude Akins,
Lee Van Cleef. Anthony Caruso, Paul Birch, George
Dunn, Steve Darrell, Rita Lynn, Gregg Barton,
Anthony Jochim, Jeane Wood, Juney Ellis.

DEATH IN SMALL DOSES (ALLIED ARTISTS)
Producer, Richard Heermance; Director, Joseph
Newman; Screenplay by John McGreevey; Based
on Story by Arthur L. Davis; Assistant Director,
Austen Jewell; Music by Emil Newman and Robert
Wiley Miller; September release. CAST: Peter
Graves, Mala Powers, Chuck Connors, Merry
Anders, Robert Christopher, Roy Engel, Robert B.
Williams, Harry Lauter, Pete Kooy.

CHICAGO CONFIDENTIAL (UNITED ARTISTS)
Producer, Robert E. Kent; Director, Sidney Salkow;
Screenplay by Raymond T. Marcus; Assistant Di-
rector, Milton Carter; Music by Emil Newman;
A Peerless Production; September release. CAST:
Brian Keith, Beverly Garland, Dick Foran, Beverly
Tyler, Elisha Cook, Paul Langton, Tony George,
Douglas Kennedy, Gavin Gordon, Jack Lambert,
John Morley, Benny Burt, Mark Scott, Henry
Rowland, George Cisar, Johnny Indrisano, John
Pelletti, Joe McGuinn, Asa Maynor, Jean Deane,
Sharon Lee. Phyllis Coates, Lynne Storey, Nancy
Marlowe, Harlan Warde, John Hamilton, Jack
Kenney, Joey Ray, Tom Wade, Ralph Volkie,
Jack Carr, Carl Princi, Helen Jay, Charles Meredith,
Keith Byron, Jim Bannon, Myron Cook, Dennis
Moore, Thomas B. Henry, Frank Marlowe, Linda
Brent, Bud Lewis.

BLACK PATCH (WARNER BROS.) Producer-
Director, Allen H. Miner; Screenplay by Leo Gor-
don; Assistant Director. John Chulay; Music by
Jerry Goldsmith; Wardrobe by Byron Munson;
September release. CAST: George Montgomery,
Diane Brewster, Tom Pittman, Leo Gordon, House
Peters, Jr., Lynn Cartwright, George Trevino, Peter
Brocco, Ted Jacques, Struther Martin, Gil Rankin,
Sebastian Cabot.

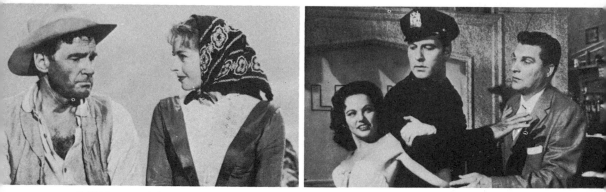

Jeff Morrow, Coleen Gray
in "Copper Sky"

Geraldine Brooks, George Montgomery
in "Street Of Sinners"

COPPER SKY (20th CENTURY-FOX) Producer,
Robert Stabler, Executive Producer-Director,
Charles Marquis Warren; Screenplay by Eric
Norden; Story by Robert Stabler; Music by Raoul
Kraushaar; Song by Raoul Kraushaar, Joe and
Marilyn Hooven; Assistant Director, Nathan R.
Barragar; A Regalscope Picture; September release.
CAST: Jeff Morrow, Coleen Gray, Paul Brinegar,
William R. Hamel, Jack M. Lomas, Strother
Martin, John Pickard, Patrick O'Moore, Rocky
Shahan, Bill McGraw, Jerry Oddo, Rush Williams,
Rodd Redwing.

STREET OF SINNERS (UNITED ARTISTS) Pro-
ducer-Director, William Berke; Screenplay by John
McPartland; Story by Philip Yordan; Music by
Albert Glasser; Song composed and played by
Danny Welton; Assistant Directors, John Bowman
and John Zane; A Security Picture; September
release. CAST: George Montgomery, Geraldine
Brooks, Nehemiah Persoff, Marilee Earle, William
Harrigan, Stephen Joyce, Clifford David, Diana
Milay, Sandra Rehn, Danny Dennis, Ted Irwin,
Melvin Decker, Lou Gilbert, Barry McGuire, Elia
Clark, Jack Hartley, Billy James, Liza Balesca,
Eva Gerson, John Holland, Bob Duffy, Joey Faye,
Fred Herrick, Charlie Jordan, John Barry, Wolf
Barzell, Stephen Elliot.

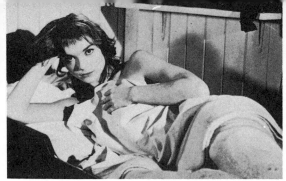

**Elsa Martinelli
in "Stowaway Girl"**

**Al Fisher, Teddy Randazzo, Lou Marks
in "Mister Rock And Roll"**

STOWAWAY GIRL (PARAMOUNT) Producer, Ivan Foxwell; Director, Guy Hamilton; Screenplay by William Woods, Guy Hamilton, Ivan Foxwell; Based on Novel by William Woods; Assistant Director, Jack Causey; Costumes by Beatrice Dawson; Music by William Alwyn; September release. CAST: Trevor Howard, Pedro Armendariz, Elsa Martinelli, Leslie Weston, Donald Pleasence, Jack McGowran, Warren Mitchell, Harcourt Curacao, Barry Lowe, Juan Carolilla, John Rae, Roger Delgado, Harold Kasket, Max Butterfield, Andy Ho, Peter Illing, Armando Guinle, Michael Peake.

MISTER ROCK AND ROLL (PARAMOUNT) Producers, Ralph Serpe and Howard B. Kreitsek; Director, Charles Dubin; Screenplay by James Blumgarten; September release. CAST: Teddy Randazzo, Lois O'Brien, Jay Barney, Allan Freed, Al Fisher, Lou Marks, Earl George, Rocky Graziano, Ralph Stantly, Lionel Hampton.

THE DEERSLAYER (20th CENTURY-FOX) Producer-Director, Kurt Neumann; Screenplay by Carroll Young and Kurt Neumann; Based on Novel by James Fenimore Cooper; Music by Paul Sawtell; In CinemaScope and DeLuxe Color; September release. CAST: Lex Barker, Rita Moreno, Forrest Tucker, Cathy O'Donnell, Jay C. Flippen, Carlos Rivas, John Halloran, Joseph Vitale, Rocky Shahan, Phil Schumacker, George Robotham, Carol Henry.

BACK FROM THE DEAD (20th CENTURY-FOX) Producer, Robert Stabler; Director, Charles Marquis Warren; Screenplay by Catherine Turney; Based on her Novel "The Other One"; Music by Raoul Kraushaar; Assistant Director, Nathan Barragar; A Regalscope Film; September release. CAST: Peggie Castle, Arthur Franz, Marsha Hunt, Don Haggerty, Marianne Stewart, Evelyn Scott, Helen Wallace, Jeane Wood, James Bell, Ned Glass, Otto Reichow, Jeanne Dates, Frances Turner, Joan Bradshaw.

SHORT CUT TO HELL (PARAMOUNT) Producer, A. C. Lyles; Director, James Cagney; Screenplay by Ted Berkman and Raphael Blau; Based on Screenplay by W. R. Burnett from a Novel by Graham Greene; Assistant Director, Richard Caffey; Costumes by Edith Head; In VistaVision; September release. CAST: Robert Ivers, Georgann Johnson, William Bishop, Jacques Aubuchon, Peter Baldwin, Yvette Vickers, Murvyn Vye, Milton Frome, Jacqueline Beer, Gail Land Dennis McMullen, William Newell, Sarah Selby, Mike Ross, Douglas Spencer, Danny Lewis, Richard Hale, Douglas Evans, Hugh Lawrence, Joe Bassett, William Pullen, Russell Trent, Joe Forte, Roscoe Ates.

FORTY GUNS (20th CENTURY-FOX) Produced, Directed, and Written by Samuel Fuller; Music by Harry Sukman; In CinemaScope; September release. CAST: Barbara Stanwyck, Barry Sullivan, Dean Jagger, John Ericson, Gene Barry, Robert Dix, Eve Brent, Jack Carroll.

**Lex Barker
in "The Deerslayer"**

**Richard Conte, Diane Foster
in "The Brothers Rico"**

ENEMY FROM SPACE (UNITED ARTISTS) Producer, Anthony Hinds; Director, Val Guest; Screenplay by Nigel Kneale and Val Guest; Story by Nigel Kneale; Music by James Bernard; Assistant Director, Don Weeks; September release. CAST: Brian Donlevy, John Longden, Sydney James, Bryan Forbes, William Franklyn, Vera Day, Charles Lloyd Pack, Tom Chatto, John Van Eyssen, Percy Herbert, Michael Ripper, John Rae, Marianne Stone, Ronald Wilson, Jane Aird, Betty Impey, Lloyd Lamble, John Stuart, Gilbert Davis, Joyce Adams, Edwin Richfield, Howard Williams, Phillip Baird, Robert Raikes, John Fabian, George Merritt, Arthur Blake, Michael Balfour.

THE BROTHERS RICO (COLUMBIA) Producer, Lewis J. Rachmil; Director, Phil Karlson; Screenplay by Lewis Meltzer and Ben Perry; Based on Story by Georges Simenon; Gowns by Jean Louis; Music by George Duning; Assistant Director, Jack Berne; September release. CAST: Richard Conte, Dianne Foster, Kathryn Grant, Larry Gates, James Darren, Argentina Brunetti, Lamont Johnson, Harry Bellaver, Paul Picerni, Paul Dubov, Rudy Bond, Richard Bakalyan, William Phipps, Mimi Aguglia, Maggie O'Byrne, George Cisar, Peggy Maley, Jane Easton.

175

John Beal, Augusta Dabney
in "That Night"

Sydney Chaplin, Fred MacMurray, John Gavin,
John Larch, Dorothy Malone in "Quantez"

NAKED IN THE SUN (ALLIED ARTISTS) Producer-Director, ·R. John Hugh; Screenplay by Frank G. Slaughter; From his Novel "The Warrior"; Assistant Director, Gayle S. DeCamp; In Eastman Color; September release. CAST: James Craig, Lita Milan, Barton MacLane, Dennis Cross, Robert Wark, Jim Boles, Tony Hunter, Douglas Wilson, Peter Dearing, Tony Morris, Mike Crecco, Bill Armstrong.

THAT NIGHT (UNIVERSAL) Producer, Himan Brown; Director, John Newland; Story and Screenplay by Robert Wallace and Jack Rowles; Associate Producer, Mende Brown; Music by Mario Nascimbene; Assistant Director, Michael Phillips; A Galahad Film; September release. CAST: John Beal, Augusta Dabney, Malcolm Brodrick, Dennis Kohler, Beverly Lunsford, Shepperd Strudwick, Rosemary Murphy, Bill Darrid, Joe Julian.

UNKNOWN TERROR (20th CENTURY-FOX) Producer, Robert Stabler; Director, Charles Marquis Warren; Screenplay by Kenneth Higgins; Music by Raoul Kraushaar; A Regalscope Film; September release. CAST: John Howard, Mala Powers, Paul Richards, May Wynn, Gerald Milton, Duane Gray, Charles Gray, Charles Postal, Patrick O'Moore, William Hamel, Richard Gilden, Martin Garralaga, Sir Lancelot.

TEENAGE DOLL (ALLIED ARTISTS) Producer-Director, Robert Corman; Executive Producer, Bernard Woolner; Associate Producer, Lawrence Woolner; Screenplay by Charles B. Griffith; Music by Walter Greene; September release. CAST: June Kenney, Fay Spain, John Brinkley, Collette Jackson, Barbara Wilson, Ziva Rodan, Ed Nelson, Sandy Smith, Barboura Morris, Richard Devon, Jay Sayer, Richard Cutting, Dorothy Neumann.

QUANTEZ (UNIVERSAL) Producer, Gordon Kay; Director, Harry Keller; Screenplay by R. Wright Campbell; Story by Anne Edwards and R. Wright Campbell; Gowns by Rosemary Odell; Assistant Director, George Lollier; Music by Herman Stein; Songs by Frederick Herbert and Arnold Hughes; In CinemaScope and Eastman Color; October release. CAST: Fred MacMurray, Dorothy Malone, James Barton, Sydney Chaplin, John Gavin, John Larch, Michael Ansara.

PANAMA SAL (REPUBLIC) Producer, Edward J. White; Director, William Witney; Screenplay by Arnold Belgard; Assistant Director, Ben Bishop; Songs by Joe and Marilyn Hooven; Choreography by Roland Dupree; A Vineland Production in Naturama; October release. CAST: Elena Verdugo, Edward Kemmer, Carlos Rivas, Harry Jackson, Joe Flynn, Christine White, Albert Carrier, Jose Gonzales Gonzales, Billie Bird, Ukonu and His Afro-Calypsonians.

Cornel Wilde, Jean Wallace, Larry Pennell
in "The Devil's Hairpin"

Lili Gentle, Mark Damon
in "Young And Dangerous"

THE DEVIL'S HAIRPIN (PARAMOUNT) Producer-Director, Cornel Wilde; Screenplay by James Edmiston and Cornel Wilde; Assistant Director, Bernard McEveety, Jr.; Costumes by Edith Head; Songs by Ross Bagdasarian, and by Van Cleave; A Theodora Production in Technicolor and Vista-Vision; October release. CAST: Cornel Wilde, Jean Wallace, Arthur Franz, Mary Astor, Paul Fix, Larry Pennell, Gerald Milton, Ross Bagdasarian, Morgan Jones, Jack Kosslyn, Jack Latham, Gil Stuart, George Gilbreth, Mabel Lillian Rea, Gordon Mills, Sue England, Dorene Porter, John Benson.

YOUNG AND DANGEROUS (20th CENTURY-FOX) Producer-Director, William F. Claxton; Associate Producer, William J. Magginetti; Screenplay by James Landis; Music by Paul Dunlap; Assistant Director, Clancy Herne; A Regal Films Production; October release. CAST: Mark Damon, Lili Gentle, Eddie Binns, Frances Mercer, Ann Doran, George Brenlin, Jerry Barclay, William Stevens, Connie Stevens, Danny Welton, Shirley Falls, Ronald Foster, Bill Shannon, Marlyn Carrol, Joan Bradshaw, Marion Collier, June Burt, James Canino, Bill Boyett, Don Devlin, Paul Bryar, Buddy Mason, Judy Bamber, Kim Scala, Doris Kemper, Brandy Bryan, Roy Darmour, Ron Barbanell, Clancy Herne.

176

Virginia Field, Gary Vinson, Judy Busch
in "Rockabilly Baby"

Rory Calhoun, Yvette Dugay, Eugene Iglesias
in "Domino Kid"

ROCKABILLY BABY (20th CENTURY-FOX) Producer-Director, William F. Claxton; Associate Producer, William J. Magginetti; Screenplay by Will George and William Driskill; Songs by Paul Dunlap; Sung by Luis Amando; "Teenage Cutie" by Dick Kallman; Assistant Director, Nat Merman; A Regalscope Picture; October release. CAST: Virginia Field, Douglas Kennedy, Les Brown, Irene Ryan, Ellen Corby, Lewis Martin, Norman Leavitt, Gene Roth, June Jocelyn, Mary Benoit, Hazel Shermet, Renny McEvoy, Tony Marshall, James Goodwin, Ken Miller, Jimmy Murphy, Barry Truex, Sandy Wirth, Cindy Robbins, Susan Easter, Barbara Gayle, Susan Volkmann, Caryl Volkmann, Judy Busch, Marlene Willis, Gary Vinson, Phil Tead, Watson Downs, Frank Marlowe, Frank Sully, Ronald Foster, Fred Darian.

GUN BATTLE AT MONTEREY (ALLIED ARTISTS) Executive Producer, D. Jersey Grut; Producer, Carl K. Hittleman; Director, Sidney Franklin, Jr.; Screenplay by Jack Leonard, Lawrence Resner and David Lang; Assistant Directors, Russell Ray Heinze and Sam Schneider; A C.B. Film; Wardrobe by Allan Sloane; October release. CAST: Sterling Hayden, Ted de Corsia, Pamela Duncan, Mary Beth Hughes, Lee Van Cleef, Charles Cane, Byron Foulger, I. Stanford Jolley, Pat Comiskey, Mauritz Hugo, Fred Sherman, George Baxter, Michael Vallon, John Dalmer.

DOMINO KID (COLUMBIA) Producers, Rory Calhoun and Victor M. Orsatti; Director, Ray Nazarro; Screenplay by Kenneth Gamet and Hal Biller; Story by Rory Calhoun; Assistant Director, Floyd Joyer; October release. CAST: Rory Calhoun, Kristine Miller, Andrew Duggan, Yvette Dugay, Peter Whitney, Eugene Iglesias, Robert Burton, Bart Bradley, James Griffith, Roy Barcroft, Denver Pyle, Ray Corrigan, Wes Christensen, Don Orlando.

THE BLACK SCORPION (WARNER BROS.) Producers, Frank Melford and Jack Dietz; Director, Edward Ludwig; Screenplay by David Duncan and Robert Blees; Story by Paul Yawitz; Music by Paul Sawtell; Assistant Directors, Ray Heinze and Jaime Contreras; October release. CAST: Richard Denning, Mara Corday, Carlos Rivas, Mario Navarro, Carlos Muzquiz, Pascual Pena, Fanny Schiller, Pedro Galvan, Arturo Martinez.

THE INVISIBLE BOY (M-G-M) Producer, Nicholas Nayfack; Director, Herman Hoffman; Screenplay by Cyril Hume; Story by Edmund Cooper; Music by Les Baxter; Assistant Director, Bert Chervin; A Pan Production; October release. CAST: Richard Eyer, Philip Abbott, Diane Brewster, Harold J. Stone, Robert Harris, Dennis McCarthy, Alexander Lockwood, John O'Malley, Gage Clark, Than Wynn, Jefferson Dudley Searles, Alfred Linder, Ralph Votrian, Michael Miller.

Sterling Hayden, Pamela Duncan
in "Gun Battle At Monterey"

Ron Randell, Mamie Van Doren
in "The Girl In Black Stockings"

HELL BOUND (UNITED ARTISTS) Executive Producer, Aubrey Schenck; Producer, Howard W. Koch; Director, William Hole, Jr.; Screenplay by Richard Landau; Music by Les Baxter; Story by Richard Landau and Arthur Orloff; Assistant Director, Paul Wurtzel; A Bel-Air Production; October release. CAST: John Russell, June Blair, Stuart Whitman, Margo Woode, George Mather, Stanley Adams, Gene O'Donnell, Frank Fenton, Virginia DeLee, Dehl Berti, Sammee Tong, Charles Webster, Edward ReRoo, Marge Evans, Ann Daro, Frank McGrath, Kay Garrett, Bob Strong, George Mayon, Red Morgan, Dick Standish, William Flaherty, George H. Whiteman, Richard Martin, Jerry Frank, Larry Thor, Scott Peters.

THE GIRL IN BLACK STOCKINGS (UNITED ARTISTS) Executive Producer, Aubrey Schenck; Director, Howard W. Koch; Screenplay by Richard Landau; Story by Peter Godfrey; Music by Les Baxter; Assistant Director, Don Torpin; A Bel-Air Production; October release. CAST: Lex Barker, Anne Bancroft, Mamie Van Doren, Ron Randell, Marie Windsor, John Dehner, John Holland, Diana Vandervlis, Richard Cutting, Larry Chance, Gene O'Donnell, Gerald Frank, Karl MacDonald, Norman Leavitt, David Wright, Mark Bennett, Stuart Whitman, Mickey Whiting.

177

Peter Cushing, Forrest Tucker
in "The Abominable Snowman"

James Darren, Joy Stoner
in "Tiajuana Story"

THE ABOMINABLE SNOWMAN (20th CEN-
TURY-FOX) Producer, Aubrey Baring; Director,
Val Guest; Screenplay by Nigel Kneale; Based on
His Play "THE CREATURE"; A Regal Films
Production; October release. CAST: Forrest
Tucker, Peter Cushing, Maureen Connell, Richard
Wattis, Robert Brown.

WOMAN IN A DRESSING GOWN (WARNER)
BROS.) Producers, Frank Godwin and J. Lee
Thompson; Director, J. Lee Thompson; Story and
Screenplay by Ted Willis; Assistant Director,
Frederic Goode; October release. CAST: Yvonne
Mitchell, Sylvia Syms. Anthony Quayle, Andrew
Ray, Olga Lindo, Harry Locke, Marianne Stone,
Michael Ripper, Max Butterfield, Roberta Woolley,
Melvyn Hayes, Cordelia Mitchell, Carole Lesley.

HELL CANYON OUTLAWS (REPUBLIC) Pro-
ducer, T. Frank Woods; Director, Paul Landres;
Screenplay by Allan Kaufman and Max Glandbard;
Music by Irving Gertz; Song composed and sung
by Dick Kallman; Assistant Director, Maurice
Vaccarino; October release. CAST: Dale Robert-
son, Brian Keith, Rossana Rory. Dick Kallman,
Don Megowan, Mike Lane, Buddy Baer, Charles
Fredericks, Alexander Lockwood, James Nusser,
James Maloney, William Pullen, George Ross,
George Pembroke, Vincent Padula, Tom Hubbard.

LOOKING FOR DANGER (ALLIED ARTISTS)
Producer, Ben Schwalb; Director, Austen Jewell;
Screenplay by Elwood Ullman; Story by Elwood
Ullman and Edward Bernds; Assistant Director,
Richard Bermerkamp; Music by Marlin Skiles;
Wardrobe by Bert Henrikson; October release.
CAST: Huntz Hall, Stanley Clements, Lili Kardell,
David Gorcey, Jimmy Murphy, Eddie LaRoy,
Peter Mamakos, Richard Avonde, Michael Granger,
George Khoury, Henry Rowland, Otto Reichow.

THE TIAJUANA STORY (COLUMBIA) Producer,
Sam Katzman; Director, Leslie Kardos; Screenplay
by Lou Morheim; Assistant Director, Leonard
Katzman; A Clover Production; October release.
Cast: Rodolfo Acosta, James Darren, Robert
McQueeney, Jean Willes, Joy Stoner, Paul Newlan,
George E. Stone, Michael Fox, Robert Blake,
William Fawcett, Ric Vallin, Ralph Valencia,
Susan Seaforth, William Tannen, Susan Ridgeway,
Paul Coates.

SORORITY GIRL (AMERICAN-INTERNATION-
AL) Executive Producer, James H. Nicholson;
Producer-Director, Roger Corman; Screenplay by
Ed Waters and Leo Lieberman; Assistant Director,
Jack Bohrer; Music by Ronald Stein; October re-
lease. CAST: Susan Cabot, Dick Miller, Barboura
O'Neill, June Kenney, Barbara Crane, Fay Baker,
Jeane Wood.

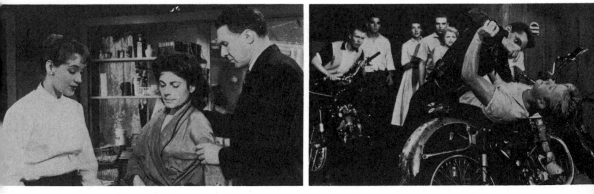

Sylvia Syms, Yvonne Mitchell, Anthony Quayle,
in "Woman In A Dressing Gown"

John Ashley, Steve Terrell
in "Motorcycle Gang"

AFFAIR IN HAVANA (ALLIED ARTISTS) Pro-
ducer, Richard Goldstone; Director, Laslo Benedek;
Screenplay by Burton Lane and Maurice Zimm;
Story by Janet Green; Assistant Director, Mark
Evans; Music by Ernest Gold; Songs by Alberto
Zayas Govin; A Dudley Pictures International
Corp. of Cuba Production; October release. CAST:
John Cassavetes. Raymond Burr, Sara Shane, Lilia
Lazo, Sergio Pena, Celia Cruz, Jose Antonio
Rivero, Miguel Angel Blanco.

MOTORCYCLE GANG (AMERICAN-INTERNA-
TIONAL) Executive Producer, Samuel Z. Arkoff;
Producer, Alex Gordon; Director, Edward L. Cahn;
Story and Screenplay by Lou Rusoff; Music by
Albert Glasser; A Golden State Production; October
release. CAST: Anne Neyland, Steve Terrell, John
Ashley, Carl Switzer, Raymond Hatton, Russ
Bender, Jean Moorhead, Scott Peters, Eddie Kafa-
fian, Shirley Falls, Aki Aleong, Wayne Taylor,
Hal Bogart, Phyllis Cole, Suzanne Sydney, Edmund
Cobb, Paul Blaisdell, Zon Murray, Felice Rich-
mond.

Lowell Brown, Audrey Totter, James Craig
in "Ghost Diver"

John Archer, Randolph Scott, Noah Beery, Jr.
in "Decision At Sundown"

HEAR ME GOOD (PARAMOUNT) Produced, Directed and Written by Don McGuire; Costumes by Edith Head; Assistant Director, Richard Caffey; In VistaVision; October release. CAST: Hal March, Joe E. Ross, Merry Anders, Jean Willes, Milton Frome, Joey Faye, Richard Bakalyan, Tom Duggan.

GHOST DIVER (20th CENTURY-FOX) Producer, Richard Einfeld; Written and Directed by Richard Einfeld and Merrill G. White; Music by Paul Sawtell and Bert Shefter; Associate Producer and Assistant Director, Ralph J. Slosser; A Regalscope Picture; October release. CAST: James Craig, Audrey Totter, Pira Louis, Nico Minardos, Lowell Brown, Rodolfo Hoyos, Jr., George Trevino, Elen Ca Vinci, Paul Stader, Diane Webber, Robert Lorenz, Richard Geary, Tom Garland, Michael Dugan.

THE TALL STRANGER (ALLIED ARTISTS) Producer, Walter Mirisch; Associate Producer, Richard Heermance; Director, Thomas Carr; Screenplay by Christopher Knopf; Story by Louis L'Amour; Assistant Director, Austen Jewell; Music by Hans Salter; In CinemaScope and DeLuxe Color; November release. CAST: Joel McCrea, Virginia Mayo, Barry Kelley, Michael Ansara, Whit Bissell, James Dobson, George Neise, Leo Gordon, Michael Pate, Adam Kennedy, Ray Teal, Philip Phillips, Robert Foulk, Jenifer Lea, George J. Lewis, Guy Prescott, Ralph Reed.

DECISION AT SUNDOWN (COLUMBIA) Producer, Harry Joe Brown; Associate Producer, Randolph Scott; Director, Budd Boetticher; Screenplay by Charles Lang, Jr.; Story by Vernon L. Fluharty; Assistant Director, Sam Nelson; Music by Heinz Roemheld; In Technicolor; November release. CAST: Randolph Scott, John Carroll, Karen Steele, Valerie French, Noah Beery, John Archer, Andrew Duggan, James Westerfield, John Litel, Ray Teal, Vaughn Taylor, Richard Deacon, H. M. Wynant, Guy Wilkerson.

RAIDERS OF OLD CALIFORNIA (REPUBLIC) Producer-Director, Albert C. Gannaway; Associate Producers and Screenplay by Sam Roeca and Thomas G. Hubbard; Assistant Director, Les Guthrie; November release. CAST: Jim Davis, Arleen Whelan, Faron Young, Marty Robbins, Lee Van Cleef, Louis Jean Heydt, Harry Lauter, Douglas Fowley, Larry Dobkin, Bill Coontz, Don Diamond, Ric Vallon, Tom Hubbard.

THE CROOKED CIRCLE (REPUBLIC) Producer, Rudy Ralston; Director, Joe Kane; Screenplay by Jack Townley; Assistant Director, Leonard Kunody; A Ventura Production in Naturama; November release. CAST: John Smith, Fay Spain, Steve Brodie, Don Kelly, Robert Armstrong, John Doucette, Philip Van Zandt, Richard Karlan, Bob Swan, Don Haggerty, Peter Mamakos.

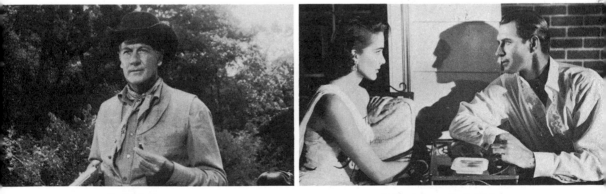

Joel McCrea
in "The Tall Stranger"

Julie Adams, Jock Mahoney
in "Slim Carter"

UNDER FIRE (20th CENTURY-FOX) Producer, Plato Skouras; Director, James B. Clark; Screenplay by James Landis; Music by Paul Dunlap; A Regalscope Production; November release. CAST: Rex Reason, Henry Morgan, Steve Brodie, Peter Walker, Robert Levin, Jon Locke, Gregory La-Fayette, Karl Lukas, Frank Gerstle, Tom McKee, John Murphy, Edmund Penney, Seymour Green, Dave Tomack, Walter Maslow, David Carlisle, William Allyn, Rita Paul, Kay Kuter, Keith Byron, Neyle Morrow, K. L. Smith, Robert Hinkle, Robert Colbert, Al Shelley, Troy Patterson, Dehl Berti, Ronald Foster, Sid Melton, George Chakiris, Ed Hinton, Nico Minardos, Calvin Booth, Lorraine Martin, Mary Townsend.

SLIM CARTER (UNIVERSAL) Producer, Howie Horwitz; Director, Richard Bartlett; Screenplay by Montgomery Pittman; Story by David Bramson and Mary C. McCall, Jr.; Gowns by Bill Thomas; Assistant Director, William Holland; Music by Herman Stein; Songs by Ralph Freed and Beasley Smith, Jimmy Wakely and Joseph Gershenson; In Eastman Color; November release. CAST: Jock Mahoney, Julie Adams, Tim Hovey, William Hopper, Ben Johnson, Joanna Moore, Walter Reed, Maggie Mahoney, Roxanne Arlen, Jim Healy, Bill Williams, Barbara Hale.

179

"I Was A Teenage Frankenstein"

Victor Mature, Diana Dors
in "The Long Haul"

I WAS A TEENAGE FRANKENSTEIN (AMERI-CAN-INTERNATIONAL) Producer, Herman Cohen; Director, Herbert L. Stock; Story and Screenplay by Kenneth Langtry; Assistant Director, Austen Jewell; Music by Paul Dunlap; November release. CAST: Whit Bissell, Phyllis Coates, Robert Burton, Gary Conway, George Lynn, John Cliff, Marshall Bradford, Claudia Bryar, Angela Blake, Russ Whitman, Charles Seel, Paul Keast, Gretchen Thomas, Jay Stoner, Larry Carr, Pat Miller.

ESCAPE FROM SAN QUENTIN (COLUMBIA) Producer, Sam Katzman; Director, Fred F. Sears; Screenplay by Raymond T. Marcus; Music by Laurindo Almeda; Assistant Director, Leonard Katzman; Song by Johnny Desmond; A Clover Production; November release. CAST: Johnny Desmond, Merry Anders, Richard Devon, Roy Engel, William Bryant, Ken Christy, Larry Blake, Don Devlin, Victor Millan, John Merrick, Norman Fredric, Barry Brooks, Lennie Smith.

BLOOD OF DRACULA (AMERICAN-INTERNA-TIONAL) Producer, Herman Cohen; Director, Herbert L. Stock; Story and Screenplay by Ralph Thornton; Assistant Director, Austen Jewell; Music by Paul Dunlap; Song by Jerry Blaine; November release. CAST: Sandra Harrison, Louise Lewis, Gail Ganley, Jerry Blaine, Heather Ames, Malcom Atterbury, Mary Adams, Don Devlin, Thomas B. Henry, Jeanne Dean, Richard Devon, Paul Maxwell, Carlyle Mitchell, Shirley DeLancey, Michael Hall.

THUNDER OVER TANGIER (REPUBLIC) Producer, W. G. Chalmers; Director, Lance Comfort; Story and Screenplay by P. Manning O'Brine; Assistant Director, George Pollard; A Sunset Palisades Production; November release. CAST: Robert Hutton, Lisa Gastoni, Martin Benson, Leonard Sachs, Derek Sydney, Emerton Court, Richard Shaw, Robert Raglan, Harold Berens, Jack Allen, Marianne Stone, Michael Balfour, Frank Forsyth, Reginald Hearn, Alex Gallier, Fred Lake, Frank Singuineau.

EIGHTEEN AND ANXIOUS (REPUBLIC) Executive Producer, Irving H. Levin; Producer, Edmond Chevie; Director, Joe Parker; Music by Leith Stevens; Songs by Phil Tuminello; Screenplay by Dale and Katherine Eunson; AB-PT Picture; November release. CAST: Mary Webster. William Campbell, Martha Scott, Jackie Loughery, Jim Backus, Ron Hagerthy, Jackie Coogan, Damian O'Flynn, Katherine Barrett, Charlotte Wynters, Yvonne Craig, Joyce Andre, Slick Slavin, Benny Rubin.

GUNFIRE AT INDIAN GAP (REPUBLIC) Producer, Rudy Ralston; Director, Joe Kane; Screenplay by Barry Shipman; Assistant Director, Leonard Kunody; A Ventura Production in Naturama; December release. CAST: Vera Ralston, Anthony George, George Macready, Barry Kelley, John Doucette, George Keymas, Chubby Johnson, Glenn Strange, Daniel White, Steve Warren, Chuck Hicks.

Richard Devon, Johnny Desmond,
William Bryant in "Escape From San Quentin"

Arthur O'Connell, Nancy Malone
in "The Violators"

RIDE A VIOLENT MILE (20th CENTURY-FOX) Producer, Robert Stabler; Story and Direction by Charles Marquis Warren, Executive Producer; Screenplay by Eric Norden; Music by Raoul Kraushaar; Assistant Director, Nathan Barragar; A Regalscope Picture; November release. CAST: John Agar, Penny Edwards, John Pickard, Richard Shannon, Charles Gray, Bing Russell, Helen Wallace, Richard Gilden, Sheb Wooley, Patrick O'Moore, Rush Williams, Roberto Contreras, Eve Novak, Mary Townsend, Dorothy Schuyler, Rocky Shahan, Norman Cram, Karl MacDonald.

THE VIOLATORS (UNIVERSAL) Producer, Himan Brown; Associate Producer, Mende Brown; Director, John Newland; Music by Elliot Lawrence; Screenplay by Ernest Pendrell; Based on Novel by Israel Beckhardt with Wenzell Brown; An RKO Picture and Galahad Production; December release. CAST: Arthur O'Connell, Nancy Malone, Fred Beir, Clarice Blackburn, Henry Sharp, Mary Michael, Joe Julian, Bill Darrid, Sheila Copelan, Bernie Lenrow, Martin Freed, Mercer McLeod, Eva Stern, Norman Rose, Maxine Stewart, Margaret Draper, Frank Maxwell, John McGovern, Norman Feld, Tom Middleton.

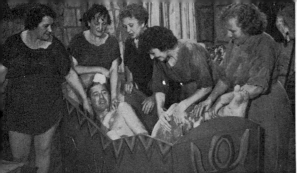

Don Taylor
in "Love Slaves Of The Amazon"

Guy Madison
in "The Hard Man"

LOVE SLAVES OF THE AMAZON (UNIVERSAL) Produced, Directed and Written by Curt Siodmak; Associate Producer, Terry Morse; Assistant Director, Rex Endsleigh; Choreography by David and Fernanda Condi; Song by Radames Gnattali; Sung by Jara Lex; In Eastman Color; December release. CAST: Don Taylor, Gianna Segale, Eduardo Ciannelli, Harvey Chalk, John Herbert, Wilson Vianna, Eugenio Carlos, Anne Marie Nabuco, Tom Payne, Gilda Nery, Louis Serrano.

THE LONG HAUL (COLUMBIA) Producer, Maxwell Setton; Direction and Screenplay by Ken Hughes; Based on Novel by Mervyn Mills; Associate Producer, Tom Morahan; Assistant Directors, Fred Slark and Ronnie Spencer; Music by Trevor Duncan; December release. CAST: Victor Mature, Diana Dors, Patrick Allen, Gene Anderson, Peter Reynolds, Liam Redmond, John Welsh, Meier Tzelniker, Michael Wade, Dervis Ward, Murray Kash, Gwen Solon, Jameson Clark, Wensley Pithey.

MAN ON THE PROWL (UNITED ARTISTS) Produced and Written by Jo and Art Napoleon; Director, Art Napoleon; Music by Ernest Gold; Associate Producer, Arthur H. Jacobs; Assistant Directors, William Farella and Robert Templeton; A Jana Production; December release. CAST: Mala Powers, James Best, Ted De Corsia, Jerry Paris, Vivi Jannis, Josh Freeman, Jeff Freeman, Peggy Maley, Eugenia Paul, Bob Yeakel.

THE HARD MAN (COLUMBIA) Executive Producer, Wallace MacDonald; Producer, Helen Ainsworth; Director, George Sherman; Screenplay by Leo Katcher, Based on His Novel; Assistant Director, Floyd Joyer; In Technicolor; December release. CAST: Guy Madison, Valerie French, Lorne Greene, Barry Atwater, Robert Burton, Rudy Bond, Trevor Bardette, Renata Vanni, Rickie Sorenson, Frank Richards, Myron Healev Robert B. Williams.

PLUNDER ROAD (20th CENTURY-FOX) Producers, Leon Chooluck and Laurence Stewart; Director, Hubert Cornfield; Screenplay by Steven Ritch; Story by Steven Ritch and Jack Charney; A Regalscope Picture; December release. CAST: Gene Raymond. Jeanne Cooper, Wayne Morris, Elisha Cook, Stafford Repp, Steven Ritch, Nora Hayden, Helene Heigh, Harry Tyler, Paul Harber, Don Garrett, Michael Fox, Richard Newton, Charles Conrad, Jim Canino, Robin Riley, Douglas Bank.

THE MONOLITH MONSTERS (UNIVERSAL) Producer, Howard Christie; Director, John Sherwood; Screenplay by Norman Jolley and Robert M. Fresco; Story by Jack Arnold and Robert M. Fresco; Gowns by Marilvn Sotto; Assistant Director, Joseph E. Kenny; December release. CAST: Grant Williams, Lola Albright, Les Tremayne, Trevor Bardette, Phil Harvey, William Flaherty, Harry Jackson, Richard Cutting, Linda Scheley, Dean Comer, Steve Darrell.

Gary Murray, Brian Donlevy
in "Escape From Red Rock"

Grant Williams, Trevor Bardette, William Flaherty, Richard Cutting in "The Monolith Monsters"

ESCAPE FROM RED ROCK (20th CENTURY-FOX) Producer, Bernard Glasser; Direction and Screenplay by Edward Bernds; Music by Les Baxter; Assistant Director, Leonard Shapiro; A Regalscope Film; December release. CAST: Brian Donlevy, Jay C. Flippen, Eilene Janssen, Gary Murray, Nesden Booth, Myron Healey, Bill Phipps, Cort Sheppard, Dan White, Tina Menard, Vincent Padulla, Elena Davinci, Linda Dangcil, Zon Murray, Frosty Royce, Al Baffert, Joe Becker, Frank Marlowe, Eileene Stevens, Frank Richards, Bud Osborne, Rick Vallin, Ed Hinton, Hank Patterson, Adamson Twins.

THE DALTON GIRLS (UNITED ARTISTS) Producer, Howard W. Koch; Executive Producer, Aubrey Schenck; Director, Reginald LeBorg; Screenplay by Maurice Tombragel; Music by Les Baxter; Story by Herbert Purdum; Song by Les and Jim Baxter; Assistant Director, Paul Wurtzel; A Bel-Air Production; December release. CAST: Merry Anders, Lisa Davis, Penny Edwards Sue George, John Russell, Ed Hinton, Glenn Dixon, Johnny Western, Malcolm Atterbury, Douglas Henderson, Kevin Enright, Al Wyatt, H. E. Willmering, Red Morgan, K. C. MacGregor, David Swapp.

Gene Raymond, Wayne Morris, Steven Ritch
in "Plunder Road"

Huntz Hall, Stanley Clements
in "In The Money"

THE FIGHTING WILDCATS (REPUBLIC) Executive Producer, Bill Luckwell; Producers, Derek Winn and Kay Luckwell; Screenplay by Norman Hudis; Based on Story by Lance Hargreaves and Norman Hudis; Director, Keefe Brasselle; Assistant Director, Stanley Goulder; An Amalgamated Production; December release. CAST: Keefe Brasselle, Kay Callard, Karel Stepanek, Ursula Howells, Bruce Seton, Sheldon Lawrence, Maya Koumani, Richard Shaw, Alex Gallier.

HELL SHIP MUTINY (REPUBLIC) Executive Producer, Jon Hall; Associate Producer, George Bilson; Directors, Lee Sholem and Elmo Williams; Screenplay by DeVallon Scott and Wells Root; Music by Paul Sawtell and Bert Shefter; Assistant Directors, Byron Roberts and Jack McEdwards; A Lovina Production; December release. CAST: Jon Hall, John Carradine, Peter Lorre, Roberta Haynes, Mike Mazurki, Charles Mauu, Stanley Adams, Danny Richards, Jr., Felix Locher, Peter Coe, Michael Barrett, Salvador Bagues.

IN THE MONEY (ALLIED ARTISTS) Producer, Richard Heermance; Director, William Beaudine; Screenplay by Jack Townley; Story by Elwood Ullman and Bert Lawrence; Assistant Directors, Jesse Corallo, Jr. and William R. Poole; Music by Marlin Skiles; December release. CAST: Huntz Hall, Stanley Clements, Judy Bamber, Eddie LeRoy, David Gorcey, Ric Roman, Byron Foulger, Dick Elliott, Benny Rubin, Ralph Sanford, Joe Devlin, James Flavin, Earle Hodgins, John Mitchum, Jack Mulhall, Fritz Feld, Wilbur Mack.

OREGON PASSAGE (ALLIED ARTISTS) Producer, Lindsley Parsons; Associate Producer, John H. Burrows; Director, Paul Landres; Screenplay by Jack DeWitt from Novel by Gordon D. Shirreffs; Assistant Director, Lindsley Parsons, Jr.; Music by Paul Dunlap; In CinemaScope and DeLuxe Color; December release. CAST: John Ericson, Lola Albright, Toni Gerry, Edward Platt, Judith Ames, H. M. Wynant, Jon Shepodd, Walter Barnes, Paul Fierro, Harvey Stephens.

John Ericson, Toni Gerry
in "Oregon Passage"

Sabu, Peter Mamakos
in "Sabu And The Magic Ring"

NEW DAY AT SUNDOWN (ALLIED ARTISTS) Producer, Scott R. Dunlap; Director, Paul Landres; Screenplay by George Waggner; Assistant Directors, Clark Paylow and Paul Cameron; In CinemaScope and DeLuxe Color; December release. CAST: George Montgomery, Randy Stuart, James Griffith, House Peters, Jr., Susan Cummings, Greg Barton, Kim Charney, Frank Wilcox, Phil Terry, Al Wyatt, Byron Foulger, Fred Krone, Dick Elliott, Kenneth MacDonald, Syd Sailor, I. Stanford Jolley, Tom McDonough, Ted Mapes.

SABU AND THE MAGIC RING (ALLIED ARTISTS) Producer, Maurice Duke; Associate Producer, Lonnie D'Orsa; Director, George Blair; Assistant Directors, Grayson Rogers and Ned Dobson; Screenplay by Sam Roeca; Music by Harry Sukman; Costumes by Eileen Younger; In DeLuxe Color; December release. CAST: Sabu, Daria Massey, Robert Shafto, Peter Mamakos, John Doucette, William Marshall, George Khoury, Vladimir Sokoloff, Robin Morse, Bernie Rich, Kenneth Terrell, John Lomma.

James Garner

Sandra Dee

James MacArthur

Pat Boone

Hope Lange

Joanne Woodward

Geoffrey Horne

Barry Coe

Jean Seberg

Diane Varsi

Tommy Sands

David Nelson

Suzy Parker

Grant Williams

Robert Evans

Inger Stevens

Brigitte Bardot

PLEASE! MR. BALZAC

Producer, Raymond Eger; Director, Marc Allegret; Screenplay by Roger Vadim and Marc Allegret; Released by Distributors Corporation of America.

CAST

Agnes Dumont	Brigitte Bardot
Daniel Roy	Daniel Gelin
Roger Vital	Robert Hirsch
Hubert Dumont	Darry Cowl
General Dumont	Jacques Dumesnil
Magali	Nadine Tallier

Daniel Gelin, Brigitte Bardot
Top: Mischa Auer, Brigitte Bardot

Brigitte Bardot

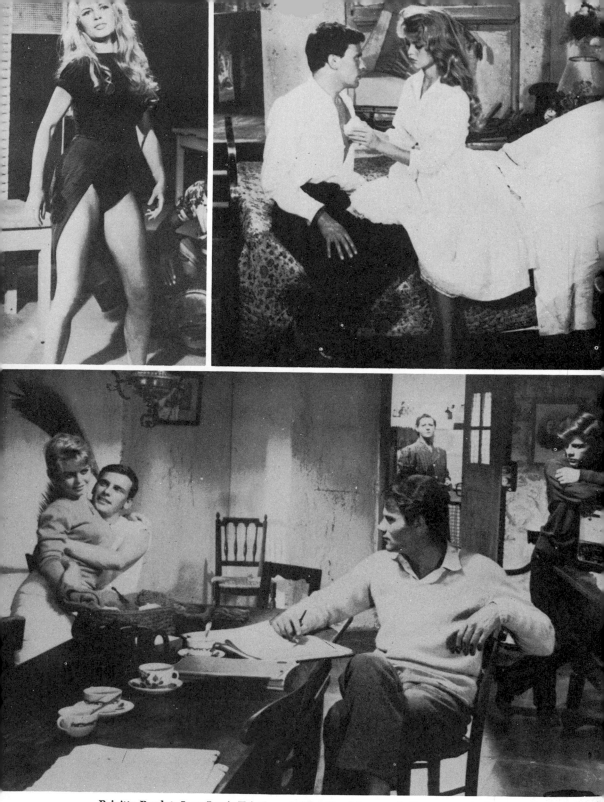

Brigitte Bardot, Jean-Louis Trintignant, Christian Marquand, Georges Poujouly
Top: Brigitte Bardot, Right with Jean-Louis Trintignant

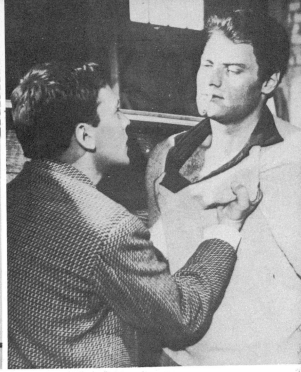

"AND GOD CREATED WOMAN"

Producer, Raoul J. Levy; Director, Roger Vadim; Screenplay by Roger Vadim and Raoul J. Levy; Music by Paul Misraki; In Cinema-Scope and Eastman Color; A Kingsley International Release.

CAST

Juliette	Brigitte Bardot
Eric	Curt Jurgens
Michel	Jean-Louis Trintignant
Antoine	Christian Marquand
Christian	Georges Poujouly
M. Vigier-Lefranc	Jean Tissier
Mme. Morin	Jane Marken
Mme. Tardieu	Mary Glory
Lucienne	Isabelle Corey
Rene	Jean Lefebvre
Perri	Philippe Grenier
Mme. Vigier-Lefranc	Jacqueline Ventura

Curt Jurgens, Brigitte Bardot
Top: Brigitte Bardot
Center: Christian Marquand, Brigitte Bardot

Jean-Louis Trintignant, Brigitte Bardot
Top: Jean-Louis Trintignant,
Christian Marquand

199

Jean Gabin, Magali Noel

RAZZIA

A Gaumont Production; Director, Henri Decoin; Screenplay by Henri Decoin and Maurice Griffe; Based on Novel by Auguste Le Breton; Released by Kassler Films.

CAST

Henri Ferret	Jean Gabin
Lisette	Magali Noel
Liski	Marcel Dalio
The Catalan	Lino Ventura
Bibi	Albert Remy
Leroux	Pierre Louis
Lea	Lila Kedrova
Decharme	Alain Nobis
Birot	Armontel
Solange Birot	Jacqueline Porel
Auguste Le Breton	Himself

Antonio Cifariello, Sophia Loren, Vittorio De Sica

SCANDAL IN SORRENTO

A Cinamascope Production in Technicolor; Director, Dino Risi; Screenplay by Ettore M. Margadonna, Marcello Girosi, Dino Risi and Vincenza Talarico; Released by Distributors Corporation of America.

CAST

Maresciallo Carotenuto	Vittorio De Sica
Donna Sofia	Sophia Loren
Donna Violante Ruotolo	Lea Padovani
Nicolino	Antonio Cifariello
Caramella	Tina Pico
Don Matteo	Mario Carotenuto
Erika	Joka Berretty
Mayor of Sorrento	Antonio La Raina

Margaret Rutherford, Donald Sinden

AN ALLIGATOR NAMED DAISY

Producer, Raymond Stross; Director, J. Lee-Thompson; Screenplay by Jack Davies; Songs by Sam Coslow; Assistant Director, Pat Marsden; Choreography by Alfred Rodrigues; In VistaVision and Technicolor; Released by Rank Film Distributors of America.

CAST

Peter	Donald Sinden
Vanessa	Diana Dors
Moira	Jean Carson
Sir James	James Robertson Justice
General	Stanley Holloway
Colonel Weston	Roland Culver
Prudence Croquet	Margaret Rutherford
Mrs. Weston	Avice Landone
Albert	Stephen Boyd
Hoskins	Richard Wattis
Valet	Henry Kendall
Alligator Judge	Michael Shepley
Notcher	Ernest Thesiger

and George Woodbridge, Wilfrid Lawson, Patrick Cargill, Ronnie Stevens, Don Cameron, George Moon, Maurice Kaufmann, Arnold Bell, Charles Carson, Myrette Morven, Joan Young, John Vere, Martin Miller, Colin Freer, Jimmy Edwards, Gilbert Harding, Frankie Howerd, Ken Macintosh and His Band.

THE LIGHT ACROSS THE STREET

Produced and Written by Jacques Gauthier; Director, Georges Lacombe; Released by United Motion Picture Organization.

CAST

Olivia	Brigitte Bardot
Marceau	Raymond Pellegrin
Pietri	Roger Pigaut
Barbette	Claude Romain
Antoine	Guy Pierrauld
Le Professeur	Jean Debucourt
Albert	Berval
Ernest	Hennery
Gaspard	Lucien Hubert
L'Amoureux	Daniel Ceccaldi

Roger Pigaut, Brigitte Bardot

MAID IN PARIS

Producer, Yvon Guezel; Director, Gaspard-Huit; Screenplay by Cecil Saint-Laurent; Released by Continental Distributing Co.

CAST

Penny Benson	Dany Robin
Antoine	Daniel Gelin
Claude	Marie Daems
Gloria Benson	Tilda Thamar
Headmistress	Mary Marquet

Dany Robin, Daniel Gelin

THE GENTLE TOUCH

A Michael Balcon Production; Associate Producer, Jack Rix; Director, Pat Jackson; Assistant Director, David Middlemas; Music by Clifton Parker; Costumes by Anthony Mendleson; In Technicolor; Released by Rank Film Distributors of America.

CAST

Jim	George Baker
Susan	Belinda Lee
Pat	Delphi Lawrence
Maureen	Adrienne Corri
Anne	Henryetta Edwards
Liz	Barbara Archer
The Matron	Diana Wynyard
Home Sister	Joan Haythorne
Sister Snow	Beatrice Varley
Theatre Sister	Joan Carol
Jessie	Mandy
Assistant Matron	Constance Fraser
Ted Russell	Christopher Rhodes

and Vivienne Drummond, Richard Leech, Newton Blick, Dandy Nichols, Mark Daly, Dorothy Alison, Joss Ambler, Olwen Brookes, Barbara Leake, Iris Russell, Enda Landor, Sylvia Bidmead, Yvonne Faithfull, Shirley Lawrence, Sally Pearce, Rosamund Waring, Tarna Gwynne, Madge Brindley, Margaret Halstan, Helene Burls, Molly Hamley Clifford, John Orchard, John Warren.

Delphi Lawrence, Christopher Rhodes, Belinda Lee

Cyril Smith, Shirley Eaton, Peggy Mount

PANIC IN THE PARLOR

A Remus Production; Producer, Jack Clayton; Director, Gordon Parry; Screenplay by Philip King and Falkland L. Cary; Presented by Distributors Corporation of America.

CAST

Emma Hornett	Peggy Mount
Henry Hornett	Cyril Smith
Shirley	Shirley Eaton
Albert	Ronald Lewis
Edie Hornett	Esma Cannon
Daphne	Joy Webster
Carnoustie Bligh	Gordon Jackson
Mrs. Lack	Thora Hird
Rev. Mr. Purefoy	Geoffrey Keen

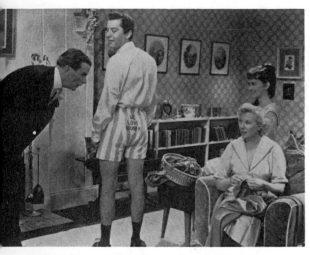

Jack Buchanan, Jerry Wayne, Brenda De Banzie, Janette Scott

AS LONG AS THEY'RE HAPPY

Producer, Raymond Stross; Director, J. Lee-Thompson; Screenplay by Alan Melville; Based on Play by Vernon Sylvaine; Executive Producer, Earl St. John; Assistant Director, Pat Marsden; Choreography by Paddy Stone and Irving Davies; Songs by Sam Coslow; Musical Score by Stanley Black; Released by Rank Film Distributors of America.

CAST

John Bentley	Jack Buchanan
Stella Bentley	Brenda De Banzie
Pat	Jean Carson
Gwen	Janette Scott
Bobby Denver	Jerry Wayne
Corinne	Susan Stephen
Pearl	Diana Dors
Barnaby	Hugh McDermott
Dr. Schneider	David Hurst
Mrs. Arbuthnot	Athene Seyler
Linda	Joan Sims
Peter	Nigel Green
Mavis	Dora Bryan
Gilbert Harding	Himself
Dancers	Paddy Stone, Irving Davies
Barmaid	Joan Hickson

and Susan Lyall-Grant, Jean Aubrey, Peter Illing, Edie Martin, Arnold Bell, Pauline Winter, Hattie Jacques, Vivienne Martin, Leslie Phillips, Charles Ross, Ronnie Stevens, Charles Hawtrey.

OEDIPUS REX

An Irving M. Lesser presentation in Eastman Color; Director, Tyrone Guthrie; William Butler Yeats version of Sophocles' tragedy; Designed by Tanya Moiseiwitsch; Released by Motion Picture Distributors.

CAST

Oedipus	Douglas Campbell
Priest	Eric House
Creon	Robert Goodier
Tiresias	Donald Davis
Jocasta	Eleanor Stuart
Man from Corinth	Tony Van Bridge
Old Shepherd	Eric House
Chorus Leader	William Hutt
Messenger	Douglas Rain

JULIETTA

Produced by Indusfilms; Director, Marc Allegret; Screenplay by Francoise Giroud; Based on Novel by Louise De Vilmorin; Released by Kingsley International.

CAST

Andre Landrecourt	Jean Marais
Julietta	Dany Robin
Rosie Facibey	Jeanne Moreau
Mme. Valendor	Denise Grey
Le Prince d'Alpen	Bernard Lancret
Martine	Nicole Berger
Arthur	Georges Chamarat
Le Commissaire	Francois Joux

Jean Marais, Dany Robin

A NOVEL AFFAIR

A Lion International Films Ltd. Production; Producer, Peter Rogers; Director, Muriel Box; Screenplay by Muriel and Sydney Box; Associate Producer, Gerald Thomas; Music by Humphrey Searle; Assistant Director, Jack Causey; Gowns by Norman Hartnell; In black and white and Eastman Color; Released by Continental Distributing Co., Inc.

CAST

Prof. Roger Winter	Sir Ralph Richardson
Sir Clement Hathaway	Sir Ralph Richardson
Judith Winter	Margaret Leighton
Leonie Hathaway	Margaret Leighton
Emily	Patricia Dainton
Betty	Patricia Dainton
Carlo	Carlo Justini
Mario	Carlo Justini
Old Woman	Ada Reeve
Maria	Andree Melly
Mr. Poldy	Frederick Piper
Miles Easter	Michael Shepley
Jimmy	Thorley Walters
Doctor	Allan Cuthbertson
Maurice	John Arnatt
Mrs. Poldy	Marjorie Rhodes
Millie	Megs Jenkins

and George Woodbridge, Barbara Archer, Michael Trubshawe, Alexander Gauge, Barbara Graley, C. Witty, Fred Tooze, Pat Ryan.

Ralph Richardson, Margaret Leighton

FERNANDEL THE DRESSMAKER

A Cite Films Production; Director, Jean Boyer; Screenplay by Gerard Carlier; Released by Union Film Distributors.

CAST

Fernand	Fernandel
Adrienne	Suzy Delair
Sophie	Francoise Fabian
Maitre Plaisant	Georges Chamarat
Picafos	Pasquali
Zwertas	Robert Destain
Apollini	Andre Bervil
The Baron	Robert Pizani

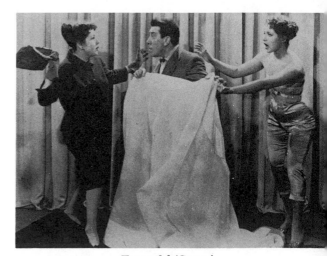

Fernandel (Center)

THE LAST BRIDGE

Cosmopol Film Production; Director, Helmut Kautner; Scenario by Helmut Kautner and Norbert Kunze; Music by Carl de Groof; Winner of David O. Selznick Golden Laurel Award, Best Actress Award to Maria Schell, Cannes Festival, International Prize, Cannes Festival; Released by Union Film Distributors in association with Joseph Rhodie.

CAST

Helga Reinbeck	Maria Schell
Boro	Bernhard Wicki
Militza	Barbara Rutting
Sgt. Martin Berger	Carl Mohner
Lt. Scherer	Horst Haechler
Momcillo	Pable Mincie
Old Peasant Woman	Tilla Durieux
English Officer	Radolcic Dragoslav
German Doctor	Robert Meyn

Maria Schell (also top left)

Jack Watling, Mercy Haystead, Gerald Harper

THE ADMIRABLE CRICHTON

A Modern Screen Play Production made at Shepperton Studios, England; Producer, Ian Dalrymple; Adapted and Directed by Lewis Gilbert; Screenplay by Vernon Harris; Based on Play by James M. Barrie; Music by Douglas Gamley; Associate Producer, Dennis Van Thal; Costumes by Bernard Nevill; Assistant Directors, Frederick Slark and W. E. Hutchinson; In Technicolor; Released by Columbia.

CAST

Crichton	Kenneth More
Tweeny	Diane Cilento
Lord Loam	Cecil Parker
Lady Mary	Sally Ann Howes
Lady Brocklehurst	Martita Hunt
Treherne	Jack Watling
Brocklehurst	Peter Graves
Ernest	Gerald Harper
Catherine	Mercy Haystead
Agatha	Miranda Connell
Vicar	Miles Malleson
Captain	Eddie Byrne
Mrs. Perkins	Joan Young
Fisher	Brenda Hogan
Rolleston	Peter Welch
Lovegrove	Toke Townley
Thomas	Roland Cupram

Maria Schell

Maria Schell (also at top)
Center: Armand Mestral

Maria Schell (Center), Suzy Delair (Right)
Top: Maria Schell, Suzy Delair
Center: Jacques Harden

GERVAISE

An Agnes Delahaie Cinematographique, Silver Films and C.I.C.C. presentation; Producer, Annie Dorfmann; Director, Rene Clement; Screenplay by Jean Aurenche and Pierre Bost; Adapted from Novel, "L'Assommoir," by Emile Zola; Music by Georges Auric; Released by Continental Distributing Co.

CAST

Gervaise	Maria Schell
Coupeau	Francois Perier
Virginie	Suzy Delair
Mme. Boche	Mathilde Casadesus
Lantier	Armand Mestral
Gouget	Jacques Harden
Adele	Ariane Lancell
M. Boche	Jacques Hilling
Pere Colombe	Andre Wasley
M. Lorilleaux	H. de LaParrent
Mme. Lorilleaux	Jany Holt
Maman Coupeau	Florelle
Nana	Chantal Gozzi
M. Gaudron	Pierre Duverger
Mme. Gaudron	Jacqueline·Morane
M. Madinier	Peignot
Mme. Fauconnier	Rachel Devirys
Zidore	Max Elbeze
Clemence	Micheline Luccioni
Mme. Bijard	Helene Tossy
Etienne at 8	Christian Denhez
Etienne at 13	Christian Ferez
Claude	Patrice Catineau

Jacques Harden, Maria Schell

Top: Maria Schell, Suzy Delair

Jean Gabin, Bourvil

FOUR BAGS FULL

A Franco-London Production; Director, Claude Autant-Lara; Screenplay by Jean Aurenche and Pierre Bost; Based on Novel by Marcel Ayme; Released by Trans-Lux Films.

CAST

Grandgil................................Jean Gabin
Martin..Bourvil
Mariette.........................Jeanette Batti
Jambier.........................Louis de Funes
and Georgette Anys, Robert Arnoux, Laurence Badie, Myno Burney, Germaine Delbat, Monette Dinay, Jean Dunet, Bernard LaJarrige, Jacques Morin, Hubert De Lapparent, Jean Verner, Hughes Wanner.

IF ALL THE GUYS IN THE WORLD . . .

An Ariane-Filmsonor-Cinetel Production; Producer, Alexander Mnouchkine; Director, Christian-Jaque; Story by Jacques Remy; Adaptation and Dialogue by H. G. Clouzot, Christian-Jaque, Jean Ferry, Jerone Geronimi, Jean Remy; Music by Georges van Parys; English titles by Herman G. Weinberg; Released by Buena Vista Film Distributing Co.

CAST
Crew of "Lutece"
Captain.............................Andre Valmy
Jos, the Mate.....................Jean Gaven
Cabin-Boy.....................Georges Poujouly
Mohammed........................Doudou Babet
Marcel.............................Marc Cassot
People in Togoland
Alberto.............................Mimo Billi
Totoche.........................Claude Sylvain
Commissioner..................Bernard Dheran
Schoolmaster.........................Andrex
Doctor Jegou..................Yves Brainville
People in Paris
Jean-Louis..............Jean-Louis Trintignant
Christine.....................Helene Perdriere
Riri.............................Jean Clarieux
People in Munich
Karl.............................Mathias Wieman
Herta.........................Gardy Granass
Johnny...........................Peter Walker
People in Berlin
Mitch.............................Charles Jarrell
Polish Air Hostess.............Margaret Rung
Norwegian Pilot....................F/O Juillard

Jean-Louis Trintignant, Helene Perdriere

Fernandel

THREE FEET IN BED

Produced in France by Sirius-S.F.F.C.; Director, Richard Pottier; Screenplay by Gerard Carlier; Released by Janus Films.

CAST
Casimir.............................Fernandel
The Artist....................Bernard La Jarrige
The Argentinian..............Germaine Montero
Casimir's Fiancee................Jacqueline Duc

WOMAN OF THE RIVER

An Italo-French Co-Production filmed at and Produced by the Ponti-De Laurentiis Studios; Producer, Basilio Franchina; Director, Mario Soldati; Story by Albert Moravia and Ennio Flaiano; Music by Angelo F. Lavagnino and Armando Trovaioli; In Technicolor; Released by Columbia.

CAST
Nives	Sophia Loren
Enzo Cinti	Gerard Oury
Tosca	Lise Bourdin
Gino Lodi	Rik Battaglia
Oscar	Enrico Olivieri

Sophia Loren, Rik Battaglia

VALUE FOR MONEY

Producer, Sergei Nolbandov; Director, Ken Annakin; Screenplay by R. F. Delderfield and William Fairchild; Based on Novel by Derrick Boothroyd; Songs by John Pritchett, Words by Peter Myers and Alec Grahame; Arranged and Danced by Paddy Stone and Irving Davies; Music by Malcolm Arnold; Assistant Director, Pat Marsden; Executive Producer, Earl St. John; In VistaVision and Technicolor; Released by Rank Film Distributors of America.

CAST
Chayley Broadbent	John Gregson
Ruthine West	Diana Dors
Ethel	Susan Stephen
Duke Popplewell	Derek Farr
Higgins	Frank Pettingell
Joy	Jill Adams
Lumm	Charles Victor
Oldroyd	James Gregson
Lord Dewsbury	Ernest Thesiger
Dancers	Paddy Stone, Irving Davies
Limpy	Donald Pleasence
Mrs. Perkins	Joan Hickson

and Hal Osmond, Sheila Raynor, Charles Lloyd Pack, Ferdy Mayne, John Glyn Jones, Leslie Phillips, Gillian Lutyens, Molly Weir, George Benson, Ronnie Stevens, Cyril Smith, Vic Wise, Ronald Chesney, Diana Munks, Eleanor Fazan, Sheila O'Neil, Aleta Morrison, Pamela Devis, Francis Pidgeon, Hermione Harvey, Jane Dore, Mavis Traill, Diana Satow, Julia Arnell, Patricia Webb, Carol Day, Mavis Greenaway, Ruth Sheill.

John Gregson, Diana Dors

PASSIONATE SUMMER

Produced by Les Films Marceau; Director, Charles Brabant; Screenplay by Charles Brabant and Maurice Clavel; Based on Play, "Island of Goats," by Ugo Betti; Released by Kingsley International.

CAST
Agatha	Madeleine Robinson
Angelo	Raf Vallone
Pia	Magali Noel
Sylvia	Dany Carrel
Eduardo	Paul Faivre

Magali Noel, Raf Vallone

ORDET

Produced by Palladium Films; Directed and Written by Carl Dreyer; Based on Play, "A Legend For Today," by Kaj Munk; Released by Kingsley International.

CAST

Morten Borgen	Henrik Malberg
Mikkel	Emil Hass Christensen
Johannes	Preben Lerdorff Rye
Anders	Cay Christensen
Inger	Birgitte Federspiel
The Doctor	Henry Skjaer
The Clergyman	Ove Rud
Peter	Ejner Federspiel

Preben Lerdorff Rye
Right: Brigitte Federspiel

Henrik Malberg
Left: Gerda Nielsen

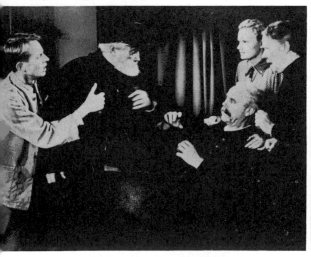

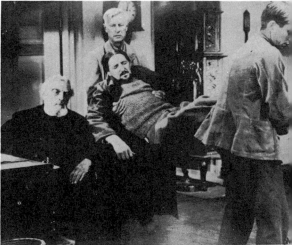

Cay Christensen, Hendrik Malberg,
Ejner Federspiel, Gerda Nielsen

Henrik Malberg, Emil Hass Christensen,
Preben Lerdorff Rye, Cay Christensen

THE RISING OF THE MOON

A Four Provinces Production; Producer, Michael Killanin; Director, John Ford; Screenplays by Frank S. Nugent; Music by Eamonn O. Gallagher; Costumes by Jimmy Bourke; Assistant Director, Dennis Bertera; Released by Warner Brothers.

CAST

Introduction..Tyrone Power

"THE MAJESTY OF THE LAW"

After the Short Story by Frank O'Connor

The Inspector..................................Cyril Cusack
The Old Man....................................Noel Purcell
The Poteen Maker..........................Jack MacGowran
Neighbors..............Eric Gorman, Paul Farrell
The Gombeen Man..........................John Cowley

"A MINUTE'S WAIT"

From the Comedy by Martin J. McHugh

Porter..Jimmy O'Dea
Station Master................................Tony Quinn
Engine Driver.................................Paul Farrell
Barmaid..Maureen Potter
Col. Frobishire...............................Michael Trubshawe
His Wife...Anita Sharp Bolster
Matchmaking Father....................Harold Goldblatt
His Boy...Godfrey Quigley
Matchmaking Aunt.......................May Craig
Her Niece..Maureen Connel
The Singer.......................................Michael O'Duffy
The Guard..J. G. Devlin
Fisherwoman...................................Ann D'Alton

"1921"

Inspired by Lady Gregory's Play "The Rising of The Moon"

The Police Sergeant......................Denis O'Dea
His Wife...Eileen Crowe
British Officer................................Frank Lawton
Black and Tan Officers...............Dennis Brennan
                                                            David Marlowe
Warder...Joseph O'Dea
Nuns...........Doreen Madden, Maureen Cusack
Sean Curran....................................Donal Donnelly
Constable...Maurice Good
Old Woman.....................................Maureen Delany
R.Q.M.S..Edward Lexy
and players from the Abbey Theatre Company

Eileen Crowe,
Denis O'Dea

Cyril Cusack (Right)

Godfrey Quigley

Denis O'Dea

Top: (L) Maureen Cusack, Doreen Madden, Frank Lawton; (R) Maureen Connel, Godfrey Quigley, May Craig, Harold Goldblatt

Henry Bookholt

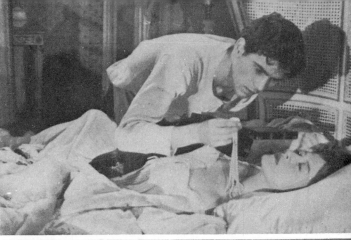

THE CONFESSIONS OF FELIX KRULL

Produced by Filmaufbau; Director, Kurt Hoffmann; Screenplay by Robert Thoeren with the cooperation of Erika Mann; Based on book by Thomas Mann; Music by Hans-Martin Majewski. Released by Distributors Corporation of America.

CAST

Felix Krull	Henry Bookholt
Zaza	Lisa Pulver
Zouzou	Ingrid Andree
Madame Houpfle	Susi Nicoletti
Professor Cuckoo	Paul Dahlke
Maria Pia	Ilse Steppat
Lord Killmarnock	Walter Rilla
Marquis de Venosta	Peer Schmidt
Schimmelpreester	Paul Henckels

Henry Bookholt, Lisa Pulver
Top: Henry Bookholt, Walter Rilla; Center: Henry Bookholt, Lisa Pulver

Henry Bookholt
Top: Henry Bookholt, Susi Nicoletti

Henry Bookholt, Susi Nicoletti

213

THE GOLD OF NAPLES

Producers, Dino De Laurentiis and Carlo Ponti; Directed by Vittorio De Sica; Screenplay by Cesare Zavattini, Vittorio De Sica and Guiseppe Marotta; Based on Novel by Giuseppe Marotta; Released by Distributors Corporation of America.

CAST

"THE RACKETEER"

The Husband	Toto
His Wife	Lianella Carrell
The Racketeer	Pasquale Cennamo

"PIZZA ON CREDIT"

The Wife	Sophia Loren
The Husband	Giacomo Furia
The Lover	Alberto Farnese
The Widower	Paolo Stoppa

"THE GAMBLER"

The Count	Vittorio De Sica
The Countess	Irene Montalto
The Boy	Piero Bilancioni
His Father	Enrico Borgstrom

"THERESA"

Theresa	Silvana Mangano
The Husband	Erno Crisa
The Intermediary	Ubaldo Maestri

Left: Sophia Loren, Giacomo Furia
Top: Erno Crisa, Silvana Mangano

DOCTOR AT LARGE

A Rank Presentation; A Betty E. Box Production made at Pinewood Studios; Director, Ralph Thomas; Screenplay by Nicholas Phipps; From the Novel by Richard Gordon; Assistant Director, Stanley Hosgood; Costumes by Yvonne Caffin; Music by Bruce Montgomery; Released by Universal-International.

CAST

Simon	Dirk Bogarde
Joy	Muriel Pavlow
Benskin	Donald Sinden
Sir Lancelot Spratt	James Robertson Justice
Nan	Shirley Eaton
Dr. Potter-Shine	Derek Farr
Bingham	Michael Medwin
Eva's Mother	Freda Bamford
Dad Ives	Abe Barker
O'Malley	John Chandos
Pascoe	George Coulouris
Sir Charles Hopcroft	Ernest Jay
Dr. Hatchett	Lionel Jeffries
Smith	Mervyn Johns
Second Examiner	Geoffrey Keen
Jasmine	Dilys Laye
Duke of Skye and Lewes	A. E. Matthews
Major	Guy Middleton
Lady Hawkins	Athene Seyler
First Examiner	Ernest Thesiger

and Martin Benson, Cyril Chamberlain, Edward Chapman, Peggyann Clifford, Campbell Cotts, Junia Crawford, Judith Furse, Gladys Henson, Anne Heywood, Charles Lloyd Pack, Harry Locke, Terence Longdon, Barbara Murray, Nicholas Phipps, Donald Pickering, Frederick Piper, Wensley Pithey Maureen Pryor, George Relph, Carol Richmond, Beth Rogan, Barbara Roscoe, Jean St. Clair, Ronnie Stevens, Michael Trubshawe, Molly Urquhart.

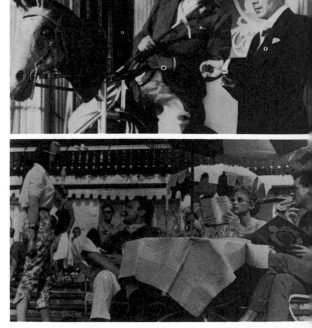

Donald Sinden, Muriel Pavlow, Dirk Bogarde
Center: A. E. Matthews, Dirk Bogarde

THE RED BALLOON

Produced, Directed and Written by Albert
Lamorisse; Released by Lopert Films. Recipient of a special award at the Cannes Film
Festival.

CAST
Little Boy_____Pascal Lamorisse
Little Girl_____Sabine Lamorisse

Pascal Lamorisse (also at top)

Martine Carol, Charles Boyer

NANA

A Roitfeld Production in color; Director, Christian Jaque; Screenplay by Jean Terry, Albert Balentin, Henri Jeanson and Christian Jaque; Adapted from the Novel by Emile Zola; Released by Times Film Corporation.

CAST

Nana	Martine Carol
Count Muffat	Charles Boyer
Count Vandeuvres	Jacques Castelot
Bordenave	Paul Frankeur
Steiner	Noel Roquevert
Fontan	Walter Chiari
Napoleon III	Jean Debucourt
Countess Muffatt	Elisa Cegani
Zoe	Marguerite Pierry
Venot	Pierre Palau

Left: John Mills, Martyn Garrett

THE BABY AND THE BATTLESHIP

Producer, Anthony Darnborough; Director, Jay Lewis; Screenplay by Jay Lewis and Gilbert Hackforth Jones; Additional Scenes and Dialogue by Bryan Forbes; Based on Novel by Anthony Thorne; In Eastman Color; Released by Distributors Corporation of America.

CAST

"Puncher" Roberts	John Mills
"Knocker" White	Richard Attenborough
Maria	Lisa Gastoni
The Baby	Martyn Garrett
Professor	Bryan Forbes
Whiskers	Harold Siddons
Sails	Clifford Mollison
Captain	Michael Hordern
Marshal	Andre Morell

Alastair Sim, John Chandos

THE GREEN MAN

Produced and Written by Sidney Gilliat and Frank Launder; Based on their Play, "Meet A Body"; Directed by Robert Day; Released by Distributors Corporation of America.

CAST

Hawkins	Alastair Sim
William Blake	George Cole
Ann Vincent	Jill Adams
Marigold	Avril Angers
Boughtflower	Terry Thomas
McKecknie	John Chandos
Lily	Dora Bryan
Reginald	Colin Gordon
Joan Wood	Eileen Moore
Sir Gregory	Raymond Huntley

THE SMALLEST SHOW ON EARTH

Producer, Michael Relph; Director, Basil Dearden; Screenplay by William Rose and John Eldridge; Based on Story by William Rose; Presented by Frank Launder and Sidney Gilliat; Released by Times Films.

CAST

Matt	Bill Travers
Jean	Virginia McKenna
Mrs. Fazackalee	Margaret Rutherford
Mr. Quill	Peter Sellers
Old Tom	Bernard Miles
Hardcastle	Francis De Wolff
Robin	Leslie Phillips
Marlene Hogg	June Cunningham

Virginia McKenna, Bill Travers

ALL AT SEA

Filmed at Ealing Studios; Producer, Sir Michael Balcon; Director, Charles Friend; Screenplay by T. E. B. Clarke; Released by M-G-M.

CAST

Captain Ambrose	Alec Guinness
Mrs. Barrington	Irene Browne
Tommy	Percy Herbert
Duckworth	Harold Goodwin
Mayor Crowley	Maurice Denham
Figg	Victor Maddern
Reggie	Martyn Woodman
June	Jackie Collins

Alec Guinness

THE SPANISH GARDENER

Executive Producer, Earl St. John; Producer, John Bryan; Director, Philip Leacock; Music by John Veale; Screenplay by Lesley Storm and John Bryan; Adapted from the Novel by A. J. Cronin; Assistant Directors, Stanley Hosgood and Harold Orton; In Technicolor; Released by Rank Film Distributors of America.

CAST

Jose	Dirk Bogarde
Nicholas Brande	Jon Whitely
Harrington Brande	Michael Hordern
Garcia	Cyril Cusack
Maria	Maureen Swanson
Robert Burton	Lyndon Brook
Carol Burton	Josephine Griffin
Leighton Bailey	Bernard Lee
Magdalena	Rosalie Crutchley
Jose's Mother	Ina De La Haye
Dr. Harvey	Geoffrey Keen
Pedro	Harold Scott

and Jack Steward, Richard Molinas, Susan Lyall Grant, John Adderley, David Lander.

Dirk Bogarde, Jon Whitely

Edith Piaf

ROYAL AFFAIRS IN VERSAILLES

Produced, Directed and Written by Sacha Guitry; In Technicolor; Presented by Times Film Corporation.

CAST

Louis XIV	Sacha Guitry
Mme. de Montespan	Claudette Colbert
Benjamin Franklin	Orson Welles
Cardinal de Rohan	Jean-Pierre Aumont
Woman of the People	Edith Piaf
D'Artagnan	Gerard Philipe
Mm. du Pompadour	Micheline Presle
Louis XV	Jean Marais
Jean Collinet	Daniel Gelin
Louison Chabray	Daniele Delorme
Louis XIV (young)	George Marchal
Comtesse de la Motte	Gaby Morlay
Louis XVI	Gilbert Boka
Marie Antoinette	Lana Marconi
Moliere	Fernand Gravet
Mme. de Maintenon	Marie Marquet

Maurizio Arena, Vittorio De Sica,
Giovanna Ralli

IT HAPPENED IN THE PARK

Produced by Astoria Films of Rome and Productions Sigma-Vog of Paris; Director, Gianni Franciolini; Screenplay by Serio Amidei; Released by Ellis Films.

CAST

Student	Anna Maria Ferrero
Teacher	Francois Perier
Lawyer	Vittorio De Sica
Girl	Giovanna Ralli
Boy	Maurizio Arena
Daughter	Giulia Rubino
Father	Eduardo De Filippo
Mother	Leda Gloria
Married Woman	Micheline Presle
Lover	Gerard Philipe
Young Lady of the Night	Eloisia Cianni
Older Lady of the Night	Franca Valeri

Marcello Mastroianni, Sophia Loren

THE MILLER'S BEAUTIFUL WIFE

A Titanus Production; Producers, Dino de Laurentiis and Carlo Ponti; Director, Mario Camerini; Screenplay by Ennio de Concini, Mario Camerini, Augusto Camerini, Alessandro Continenza; In CinemaScope and Technicolor; Released by Distributors Corporation of America.

CAST

Governor	Vittorio De Sica
Miller's Wife	Sophia Loren
Miller	Marcello Mastroianni
Governor's Aide	Paolo Stoppa
Governor's Wife	Yvonne Sanson

08/15

Screenplay by Ernst V. Saloman; Based on "The Revolt of Gunner Asch" by Hans Helmut Kirst; Directed by Paul May; Music by Rolf Wilhelm; Released by Times Films Corporation.

CAST

Private Asch	Joachim Fuchsberger
Lore Schulz	Helen Vita
Private Vierbein	Paul Bosiger
M/Sgt. Schulz	Emmerich Schrenk
Elizabeth Freitag	Eva Ingeborg Scholz
Ingrid Asch	Gundula Korte
Cpl. Kowalski	Peter Carsten
Sgt. Platzek	Hans Christian Blech
Lt. Wedelmann	Rainer Penkert
Lindenberg	Richard Glemnitz
Wunderlich	Dietrich Thoms
Werktreu	Hans Elwenspoek
Dr. Samig	Heinz Peter Scholz
Major Luschke	Wilfried Seyferth
Mr. Freitag	Herbert Kroll
Mr. Asch	Walter Klock

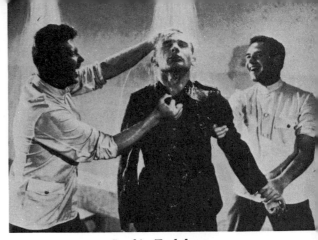

Joachim Fuchsberger

CONGRESS DANCES

A Cosmos-Neusser Production in Cinema-Scope and Trucolor; A Gloria Film; Screenplay by Kurt Nachmann; Music by Werner Richard Heymann; Assistant Director, Arnd Heyne; Costumes by Gerdago; Choreography by Willy Schulte Vogelheim; Released by Republic.

CAST

Christl Weinzinger	Johanna Matz
Alexander 1	Rudolf Prack
Uralsky	Rudolf Prack
Babette	Hannelore Bollmann
Countess Ballansky	Marte Harell
Lydia	Jester Naefe
Schoberl	Hans Moser
Franzl Eder	Josef Meinrad
Pepi Gallinger	Gunther Philipp
Count Metternich	Karl Schonbock
Bibikoff	Oscar Sima
Franz	Paul Westermeier

Johanna Matz, Rudolf Prack

CABIRIA

Producer, Dino DeLaurentiis; Director, S. Fellini; Screenplay by Federico Fellini, Ennio Flaiano and Tullio Pinelli; Released by Lopert Films.

CAST

Cabiria	Giulietta Masina
Her Lover	Francois Perier
Wanda	Franca Marzi
Jessy	Dorian Gray
The Actor	Amedeo Nazzari

Giulietta Masina

Humphrey Bogart
1899-1957

OBITUARIES

ALTON, ROBERT, 54, stage and screen dance director, died June 12, 1957, in Cedars of Lebanon Hospital, Los Angeles, of a kidney ailment. Among the films for which he directed the dance numbers were "Show Boat," "The Harvey Girls," "Bathing Beauty," "Till The Clouds Roll By," "Annie Get Your Gun" and "The Barkleys of Broadway."

ASHER, MAX, 77, pioneer film comedian, died in Hollywood, April 15, 1957. He began his career in early Universal comedies, then joined Keystone, and later worked for Famous Players, First National and Metro studios. In recent years he served as a make-up man.

BEVAN, BILLY, 70, pioneer film comic, died November 26, 1957, at his ranch home in Escondido, Calif. He began his film career in 1922 as a Keystone Kop. Other movie appearances include "Easy Pickings," "Journey's End," "The Long Voyage Home" and "Terror By Night." He retired in 1952.

BOGART, HUMPHREY, 57, screen star, died of cancer in his Beverly Hills home, Jan. 14, 1957. Famous as a screen star, he also had a long stage career which began in 1920. His film career began with the old Fox Company in "Up The River." Among his many film appearances were "Body and Soul," "Bad Sister," "Holy Terror," "The Petrified Forest," "Devil With Women," "Dead Reckoning," "The Big Sleep," "Dark Passage," "The Two Mrs. Carrolls," "The Maltese Falcon," "Treasure of The Sierra Madre," "Casablanca," "Key Largo," "Knock On Any Door," "Tokyo Joe," "Chain Lightning," "Sirocco," "The African Queen," "Deadline U. S. A.," "Beat The Devil," "The Caine Mutiny," "Sabrina," "The Barefoot Contessa," "We're No Angels," "Left Hand Of God," "The Desperate Hours," and "The Harder They Fall."

BRABIN, CHARLES J., 74, pioneer director, died of a heart attack in Santa Monica, Calif., Nov. 3, 1957. He started as a director in 1908 with the Edison Co. Later he directed for Vitagraph, Essanay, Metro, Fox, Goldwyn, Universal, M-G-M and First National. He directed many of Theda Bara's films and married her. In 1930 he retired and lived quietly with his wife until her death in 1955.

BRANTON, G. RALPH, 61, vice-president of Allied Artists, died of a heart attack in Hollywood, Dec. 2, 1957. At one time he was associated with the Monogram Pictures Corporation.

BUCHANAN, JACK, 64, British musical comedy star, died Oct. 20, 1957, in a London nursing home. Famous on the stage in both London and New York, he also appeared in English and Hollywood films. These include "Monte Cristo," "Paris," "The Band Wagon," "A Man Of Mayfair," "Good Night, Vienna," "Yes, Mr. Brown," "The French They Are A Funny Race," "The Magic Night" and "That's A Good Girl."

COSTELLO, HELENE, 53, silent film star, died Jan. 26, 1957, in Patton State Hospital, Calif. Daughter of early screen idol, Maurice Costello, with her sister Dolores, she began her career as a child film actress with the Vitagraph Co. in Brooklyn. In 1920, she began her Hollywood career with Warner Brothers. Her films include "Bobbed Hair," "The Man On The Box," "Wet Paint," "Don Juan," "In Old Kentucky," "The Circus Kid," "The Midnight Taxi," "Good Time Charlie," and the first all-talkie, "Lights of New York." Her second husband was the late Lowell Sherman.

Jack Buchanan

Billy Bevan

Helene Costello

Oliver Hardy
1892-1957

EYTHE, WILLIAM, 38, screen actor, died in Hollywood, Jan. 26, 1957. He appeared in several Broadway plays before beginning his career in motion pictures. Among his films were "Ox-Bow Incident" (his screen debut), "Song of Bernadette," "Wilson," "Wing and A Prayer," "The Royal Scandal," "Colonel Effingham's Raid," "House On 92nd Street," "Centennial Summer," "Mr. Reckless," "Meet Me At Dawn," and "Special Agent."

FORD, HARRISON, 73, former leading man of silent screen and stage, died Dec. 2, 1957, at the Motion Picture Country Hospital in California. He appeared in such films as "The Mysterious Mrs. M," "A Pair of Silk Stockings," "Such A Little Pirate," "The Third Kiss," "The Passion Flower," "Vanity Fair," "Smilin' Through," "Little Old New York," "Janice Meredith," "Up In Mabel's Room," "The Rejuvenation of Aunt Mary," "No Control," "The Wheel," "A Blonde For A Night," "The Song and Dance Man," "Rubber Tires," "Sandy," "The Rush Hour," "Primitive Lover," "The Wonderful Thing," "Wedding Bells," "Girls," "Proud Flesh," "Zander The Great."

GRIFFITH, RAYMOND, 70, film comedian and producer, died of a heart attack in Hollywood, Nov. 25, 1957. Entering the film industry in 1914, he worked as a comic for Vitagraph and Kalem companies. Later he worked with Mack Sennett, Marshall Neilan, Goldwyn and Universal before becoming a star at Paramount. Among his films, before his retirement in 1940, were "Lily Of The Dust," "Miss Bluebeard," "Forty Winks," "The Night Club," "Paths To Paradise," "A Regular Fellow," "Hands Up," "Wet Paint," "Wedding Bells," and "All Quiet On The Western Front."

HARDY, OLIVER, 65, comedian, died in North Hollywood, Calif., Aug. 7, 1957. Since 1927, he and his partner, Stan Laurel, were one of the top comedy teams of films for over two decades. Their features included "The Bohemian Girl," "Great Guns," "A Chump At Oxford," "The Bullfighters," "Way Out West," "Saps At Sea," "Babes In Toyland," "Air Raid Wardens," "Pack Up Your Troubles" and "Our Relations."

HAY, MARY, 56, former musical comedy actress, died June 4, 1957, at her home in Inverness, Calif. She appeared in several silent films including D. W. Griffith's "Way Down East," with her former husband, Richard Barthelmess.

HICKS, RUSSELL, 61, veteran actor, died of a heart attack in Hollywood, June 1, 1957. He appeared on the stage but was better known for his character roles in films. Among his recent ones were "The Bandit of Sherwood Forest," "The Maverick," "Mr. Walkie-Talkie," "Man Of Conflict," and "Seventh Cavalry." His last appearance was on the stage in "The Caine Mutiny Court Martial."

HULL, JOSEPHINE, 71, beloved stage star, died in St. Barnabas' Hospital, N. Y. C., March 12, 1957, after a long illness. She appeared in the films of several of her stage successes, including "Arsenic and Old Lace" and "Harvey" which won her an Academy Award in 1950 for best supporting actress. Burial was in the family plot in her native Newtonville, Mass.

JOHNSON, KATIE, 78, English stage and screen actress, died in Elham, Eng., May 4, 1957. Her performance in the recent film, "The Lady Killers" won her many American admirers.

JOYCE, PEGGY HOPKINS, 64, celebrated international showgirl, died of cancer, June 12, 1957, in the Memorial Hospital, N. Y. C. She appeared in one silent film, "Skyrocket," and one talkie, "International House."

LEE, JANE, 45, film actress, died in N. Y. C., March 17, 1957. With her sister, Katherine, as a child team, they starred in over 40 films for the old Fox Film Co. These included the 1914 original version of "Neptune's Daughter," "Two Little Imps," "The Troublemakers." They also appeared in vaudeville.

William Eythe

Harrison Ford

Katie Johnson

223

Norma Talmadge
1897-1957

LOCKHART, GENE, 66, screen character actor, died in St. John's Hospital, Santa Monica, Calif., March 31, 1957. His film credits include "By Your Leave," "Algiers," "The House on 92nd Street," "Leave Her To Heaven," "The Shocking Miss Pilgrim," "Foxes Of Harrow," "Joan Of Arc," "Miracle On 34th Street," "Rhubarb," "Lady From Texas," "Androcles and The Lion," "The Lady Wants Mink," "World For Ransom," "The Vanishing American," "Carousel" and "The Man In The Gray Flannel Suit."

MacBRIDE, DONALD, 63, character actor, died in Los Angeles, June 21, 1957, of a heart ailment. A Broadway stage actor, he came to Hollywood in 1938 and appeared in many films, including "Room Service," "The Seven Year Itch," "My Friend Irma," "Out Of This World," "My Sister Eileen" and "The Great Man Votes."

MAYER, LOUIS B., 72, veteran producer, and one of the founders of Metro-Goldwyn-Mayer, died in U.C.L.A. Medical Center in Los Angeles on Oct. 29, 1957, of leukemia. An immigrant boy from Minsk, Russia, with a keen business sense, imagination and eye for talent, he rose from a junk dealer in St. John and Boston to one of the most important figures in the industry.

MENZIES, WILLIAM, 60, dean of film art directors, died in his Beverly Hills home on March 5, 1957, of a heart attack. In 1928 he won an Oscar for art direction of "The Dove" and "The Tempest." His latest work was as associate producer for "Around The World In 80 Days."

MITCHELL, GRANT, 83, veteran stage and screen actor, died in Wilshire Sanitarium, Los Angeles, May 1, 1957. He starred in many Broadway plays before becoming a Hollywood character actor. His film credits include "Three On A Match," "A Midsummer Night's Dream," "Hell's Kitchen," "Edison, The Man," "The Great Lie," "My Sister Eileen," "Dixie," "Arsenic and Old Lace" and "It Happened On Fifth Avenue."

MITCHELL, RHEA, 63, silent screen actress, was found murdered in her Hollywood apartment, Sept. 16, 1957. She appeared between 1916 and 1919 as leading lady for such stars as William S. Hart, Tom Mix, King Baggott and Bert Lytell.

PATHÉ, CHARLES, 94, one of the founders of the French motion picture industry, died Dec. 25, 1957. He and his brothers founded Pathé-Cinema in 1897. In 1929 he sold his interests but many of its units still bear his name in their corporate titles. The crowing rooster, symbol of the Pathé newsreel, was familiar wherever movies were shown.

PINZA, EZIO, 64, noted Metropolitan Opera star, died May 9, 1957, at his home in Stamford, Conn. He appeared in several recent films including "Carnegie Hall," "Mr. Imperium," "Strictly Dishonorable" and "Tonight We Sing."

ROGERS, CHARLES R., 64, producer, died in Hollywood, March 29, 1957. Former vice-president of Universal, he also was head of production for the RKO-Pathe Studios, also the First National Co., and at one time he was an independent producer for both Paramount and United Artists.

SCHULBERG, B. P., 65, former film producer, died at his home in Key Biscayne, Fla., Feb. 25, 1957. He was in charge of productions for Paramount from 1925 to 1932, and since then has made many independent productions. His best known film was award-winning "Wings."

SEBASTIAN, DOROTHY, 52, film actress, died in Hollywood, April 8, 1957. She made her film bow in 1925 in Paramount's "Sackcloth and Scarlet." Later appeared in many M-G-M films including "The Single Standard," "Our Dancing Daughters," "Our Blushing Brides," "The Demi-Bride," "Spite Marriage" and "They Never Came Back."

Gene Lockhart

Louis B. Mayer

Dorothy Sebastian

Ned Sparks

Marta Toren

Erich Von Stroheim

SHEFFIELD, REGINALD, 56, film actor, died in his home in Pacific Palisades, Calif., Dec. 8, 1957. He had been active in Hollywood films since 1927. Among his many films were "Man In Halfmoon Street," "Wilson," "Man From Down Under," "Three Strangers," "Devotion," "Mr. Belvedere Goes To College" and his most recent "The Buccaneer."

SPARKS, NED, 73, stage and screen comic, died April 3, 1957, in Victorville, Calif. Prior to his retirement in 1948, he appeared in many films, including "The Big Noise," "Alias The Deacon," "The Canary Murder Case," "Strange Cargo," "Leathernecking," "The Iron Man," "The Miracle Man," "Lady For A Day," "Alice In Wonderland," "Going Hollywood," "Sweet Adeline," "Imitation Of Life," "Sweet Music," "One In A Million," "Wake Up and Live," "The Star Maker" and "Magic Town."

TALMADGE, NORMA, 61, famous film star, died at her palatial home in Las Vegas, Dec. 24, 1957. A pioneer of motion pictures, she began her career in 1910 with the Vitagraph Co. in a one reel film, "A Dixie Mother." Other early films were "A Tale Of Two Cities," "The Battle Cry Of Peace," "Missing Links," "Going Straight," "Panthea," "Poppy," "DeLuxe Annie," "The Safety Curtain," "Her Own Way," "The Forbidden City," "The Probation Wife," "The Passion Flower," "The Sign On The Door," "The Voice From The Minaret" and "The Eternal Flame." Later silent films were "Smilin' Through," "Ashes Of Vengeance," "Within The Law," "Secrets," "The Lady," "Kiki," "The Dove," "Camille" and "The Woman Disputed." She made two talkies, "New York Nights" and her last film, "DuBarry, Woman of Passion." She retired in 1930. She was married three times: to Joe Schenck, George Jessel and Dr. Carvel James who survived her. Burial was in the Hollywood Memorial Park Cemetery.

TOREN, MARTA, 30, Swedish film actress, died suddenly in Stockholm on Feb. 19, 1957. In 1947 she came to the United States where within four years she made eleven films, including "Sword of The Desert," "Casbah," "Rogues Regiment," "Illegal Entry," "One Way Street" and "Deported."

TYLER, JUDY, 24, actress, was killed July 3, 1957, in an automobile accident near Billy The Kid, Wyoming. Earlier in the year she appeared on Broadway in "Pipe Dream" and had recently completed the Elvis Presley film, "Jailhouse Rock."

VINCENT, JAMES, 74, pioneer film director, died in N. Y. C., July 12, 1957, after a long illness. He directed films for the Kalem, Fox and Pathe film companies.

VON STROHEIM, ERICH, 71, noted director and actor of the silent screen, died of cancer at his home outside Paris, May 12, 1957. Among his famous silent films were "Greed," "Merry-go-Round," "Foolish Wives" and "The Merry Widow." Among his appearances in talkies were "The Great Gabbo," "Three Faces East," "Friends and Lovers," "The Lost Squadron," "As You Desire Me," "Home Of Strangers," "The Crime Of Dr. Crespi," "The Devil Doll," "I Was An Adventuress," and "Grand Illusion" in French. His more recent films were "Five Graves To Cairo," "North Star," "Storm Over Lisbon," "Scotland Yard Investigator" and "Sunset Boulevard."

WHALE, JAMES, 60, film director, died May 29, 1957, in Hollywood. Among the pictures he directed were "Hell's Angels," "Frankenstein," "Show Boat," "Waterloo Bridge," "The Invisible Man" and "The Road Back."

WHELAN, TIM, 63, film actor, writer and director for 35 years, died Aug. 12, 1957, in Beverly Hills, Calif. He started in Hollywood in 1922 as an actor. Later he became a gag writer for Harold Lloyd and then joined Metro as a writer, director and producer.

INDEX

232

233